Club Sailor:
from back to front

Clive Eplett

Cover photo by David Hutley

Back cover photos by Neil Hardie

ISBN 978-0-9570915-0-4

Published in 2011 by Levium Books, Haslemere, GU27 1PR,
Surrey, UK.

Note: The material contained in this book is set out in good
faith for general guidance and no liability can be accepted
for loss or expense incurred as a result of relying on
particular circumstances or statements made.

Acknowledgments

I am indebted to friends, family and many members of Frensham Pond SC. It all starts with Tom, a great fleet captain who brought me into race-coaching and writing coaching articles as a consequence. This book evolved from that beginning.

Thereafter, I must thank Tim, Jeff, Judith, Jim, Neil, Chris and Sam for their feedback, Roger for pointing out where I was talking particular nonsense and David Hutley for the great cover photo. Finally to Sue and Amy for indulging me and Matthew for betting me I would never finish it.

Contents

FOREWORD

Visitors to the UK often comment on the myriad of rivers, lakes, ponds and reservoirs that litter our landscape, not forgetting our extensive coastline. Go to any one of these, however small, on a weekend from Penzance via Salcombe and the Solent to Ramsgate, Ranelagh via Oulton Mere, Hollingworth, Abersoch, Derwent reservoir then East Lothian and on to Lerwick in the Shetland Islands (all clubs I've had the pleasure of visiting) and you will almost certainly witness dinghy sailors battling around their local cans. It is these smaller clubs that provide the backbone of British sailing and the bulk of its participation. Whilst a minority of individuals just 'mess about in boats', most are out racing - pitting their skills, wits, experience and sometimes just plain luck, against the vagaries of the elements and their rivals. Many of these racers turn out weekend in, weekend out, throughout all four seasons, irrespective of what the elements conspire to throw at them. Clive is one of these, one of the regulars, a stalwart, a club benchmark. Somehow, if he is not there one weekend, everyone notices.

As UK dinghy racers, we are very lucky to have these opportunities to race on such an interesting variety of waterways. Each club has its own quirky rules, islands, mark numbering or naming systems, wind shadows, wind shifts, back eddies, waves, shallows etc. to confound us. In return, we attempt to navigate through and around these obstacles, in our never-ending quest for that perfect beat, race or day. As we get older, unlike many other sports, in sailing we continue to learn, to discover, to make new and repeat old mistakes. No two days are the same - we never tire of the battle. There's always tommorrow. "Today we were just unlucky - next weekend we'll beat him...".

'From back to front' provides a refreshing and light hearted insight into some of the techniques and approaches to both improving performance and gaining more enjoyment from your racing. Clive shares some of his wealth of experiences drawn from nearly 40 years dinghy racing, from Fowey to Frensham Pond, from single and double handers and small keelboats, but most importantly from 'the back to the front' of the fleet to address the needs of club racers. This book addresses the parts that other books ignore - it probably won't revive flagging Olympic ambitions, but it probably will get you down to your local club a few minutes earlier and may, with luck, even persuade you to dig out that road trailer and discover the delights and frustrations of all those hundreds of other clubs, many that I have been so fortunate to sample.

See you all on the water.

Roger Gilbert

Part 1
Preparatory Signal

The reason that everybody likes planning is that nobody has to do anything
Jerry Brown

PREFACE

Who the blazes is Clive Eplett and what qualifies him to write a book on sailing, you will likely ask. What has **he** won? There is a possibility you have even raced against me yourself and I only ever saw your transom in the distance.

Well, that is the point. There are many fantastic books out there, written by sailing stars with more medals and championships than you can shake a stick at. Ideal if you have the aptitude and attitude to follow in their footsteps. I read them avidly myself. Occasionally something even clicks and my sailing improves a bit as a result. But frankly, like most of us mortals, much of it does not really strike a chord or is quickly forgotten.

So this book is written by a club-racer, for club-racers.

Whilst we club sailors might occasionally pull our road trailer out of the weeds and venture forth, mostly we race at our clubs, often week in, week out, all year around. Do we really improve? Only in our dreams. In reality, if we have a good start, we will inexorably slip back towards our usual place. After a bad start we will perhaps pick a few off and still end up with a similar result.

For some this may be enough, to get away from the stresses of life for an hour or three; after all, there is nothing as wonderful as messing about in boats. But strangely, given the opportunity, the same laid-back club stalwarts will hang onto every word of a talk or new publication from a top sailor.

The books mostly assume a good-to-great start, a perfect strategy up the first beat (the experts never have running starts) thereafter consolidating and sailing away. They expect good boatspeed regardless of the conditions. They don't mention capsizing after dropping the mainsheet or because of a 60-degree header. They are silent on what to do if someone accidentally lassoes you with their mainsheet and pulls you out of your boat (laugh, keep hold of your own sheet, let go of tiller-extension) or when your mainsheet is caught by another Laser's bow and somehow looped around the leeward mark like a stern-painter (bet them they cannot do *that* again). Both of these, and more besides, have happened to me in club races.

Now, I undersell myself a bit. At my club it is rare nowadays that I am not close to, or at, the front of the fleet, whatever I sail. My coaching is well received. I can go to Opens and near half my race results can be pretty creditable. The rest? Well, I too have my frustrations. I think the sporting description for this syndrome is *flat-track-bully*. But when I got my first Laser over 20 years ago, first time out our old 470 coach, leaning on the Royal Fowey YC railings, observed that my "fore and aft trim was OK". "That the only positive thing you could see?" I asked. "Yup, 'fraid so." As ever, he was right.

Thankfully I have improved dramatically, and so can you. Believe me it is both achievable and worthwhile although the route is not necessarily the same as that for thrusting successors to Ben Ainslie, or even to my admirable club-mates Nick Craig and Roger Gilbert. Instead, the matters I am going to cover are realistic and practicable for us weekend warriors. Much is about approach and attitude – because, deep down, many club sailors sort-of know what they **should** be doing. Books have been read and talks have been attended to little effect. This book however is carefully tuned to strike the right chord for club-racers, to resonate and have a lasting impact.

A good definition of madness is continuing to do exactly the same thing over and over but each time expecting a different outcome. No sail-racer is completely bonkers, given that they have chosen sailing (the ultimate sport) but nevertheless for many the symptoms are there for all to see. It need not be this way so let's see how, together, we can improve your results.

INTRODUCTION

Aren't we lucky to have adopted the ultimate sport: racing sailing boats? Surely there is nothing to match it?

Our driving force is invisible, constantly changing in strength and direction and varies at different heights off the ground. While there is consensus about how the science works to make our boats move that science is far from perfectly understood. And that is in a wind tunnel, never mind with a rig that is moving side to side and pitching fore and aft in waves. We sail on water that moves visibly in waves but also invisibly in tides/currents and within each wave itself. Our races last sufficient time (in many cases) for meteorological changes to affect what we do.

We have a limited number of strings to pull to manipulate our sophisticated sails to the right shape (whatever the 'right shape' may be from second to second) but each control impacts another and sometimes it is not possible to get what we want from what we have, no matter what we do.

We race other boats also vying for the same wind and water and – in the process, they change the state of the wind and water too. Our racing rules are relatively complex, involving difficult judgements and are largely self-administered, mostly very successfully.

A sailing race can be gentle, but at other times it can be hugely physically demanding requiring strength, fitness and even bravery as well as co-ordination, balance and fine-motor skills. This sits alongside a cerebral challenge akin to playing chess against multiple opponents. All while standing under a cold shower of course.

Sometimes we sail in groups of two or more people, requiring leadership, management and team-working skills.

There is potential to get seriously hurt, or worse, but those occurrences are, mercifully, incredibly rare considering what we do.

We can race one against many, one against one or in teams of two, three or four, each with its own different dynamics, priorities and skill sets.

Boats come in different sizes, shapes and configurations enabling everyone to find something that suits them regardless of our individual physical traits and constraints. In many instances being male or female is irrelevant. We have a handicapping system that mostly does a reasonable job of allowing us all a fair chance to come out on top.

All these aspects interact – so being canny may offset the apparent advantages of someone taller or fitter and experience can overcome the advantages of youth.

Even if we do not want to race, there is plenty of room for enjoyment whether passage making or simply messing about on the water.

No wonder that one lifetime is insufficient to master sailing.

We club-sailors, having chosen the ultimate sport, are usually keen to partake as often as we can. Demonstrably we love our racing and we want to do well. More to the point, we want to do better, perhaps a lot better. So why do our desires rarely come true? I suggest the causes are primarily habit and inertia.

Habit and inertia seem to prevail in our modern developed world. Is that a sign of admirable contentment or a strategy to cope with the accelerating change going on all around us? Change we cannot hope to personally control?

Whatever the reason there is nothing necessarily wrong with habit and inertia. Except that we all need some contrast in our lives; an opportunity to experience the highs of an unexpected pay rise, closing a good deal or even embarking on a new romance. Perhaps this is why we race our boats: a chance to get that rush of fulfilment when we win or even just outperform expectations.

The trouble is habit and inertia cross over into our sporting lives too. We settle into a sub-optimal routine and as a result all too rarely achieve that winning high. Of course winning is not a very 'British' thing to do and there is nothing we like less than a bad winner – they are even worse than bad losers!

Deep down though, don't we want to achieve the fulfilment of sailing out of our skins and giving the rest of the fleet a good thrashing? Well what is stopping you? We know sailing is the ultimate sport, more complex than any other. That complexity gives us an opportunity to make the most of our strengths, no matter how lousy we were at PE in school. We might not be fast but we can be clever. We might not be able to straight-leg hike forever, but we could trapeze instead perhaps, or sail a non-hiking keelboat. We might not score ten out of ten on windshifts but we could well have the handyman skills, lateral thinking and subtlety of touch to produce a blindingly fast development-class machine.

This book is designed to help you shake off habits and inertia and to provide the inspiration and ideas for club sailors to radically improve their sailing. There is a lot of material here to help you make your boat better and drive it around the course in a shorter time. Unusually the first and most important section is about making your head faster. I am not a shrink or an NLP practitioner, but I am curious and I've been inspired to do some research and thinking that you can benefit from.

In Section 1 you will learn: luck is not all random chance; visualisation exercises (almost as beneficial as real-life practice) that you can do during your daily commute; out-manoeuvring evolution to embed things into long-term memory instead of forgetting them by tomorrow; the 'inner game', 'muscle memory' and interfering brains; relentlessness, the stuff of champions and more.

Such tools and insight will not just elevate you to a new performance level, but instead onto a new gradient of consistent improvement. Now that would be really useful inertia to build as a habit.

Once your head is together, Section 3 will enable you to get any ugly duckling around the course to reach its potential and Section 4 will convert that visually challenged duckling to a swan, before Section 5 helps you make it into the Usain Bolt of swans. Enough of the overdone metaphor; Section 6 then shares some wise words and provides some useful tricks and tips to bring things together.

CALL TO ACTION

This is not intended to be your typical sailing textbook. Most sailing books seem to be aimed at either beginners or those who want to be champions. Strangely, there is very little (until now) for the majority, avid weekend club-racers stuck in the middle. In a good old bell-distribution curve it looks like this:

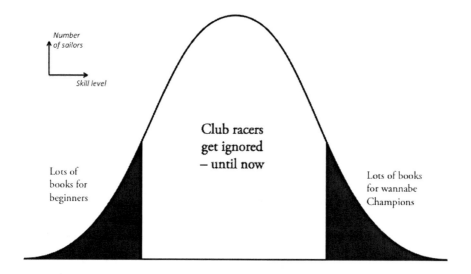

Figure 8

As a club sailor you probably know your way around many of the 'how to be a champ (like me)' books already. It is also possible that reading them improved your results hardly at all, which is a shame. But perhaps it is not surprising – they are based on a false premise. We do not need to be told **what** to do – we know that already. What we struggle with is **how** to do it. Start, spot the windshift, surf a wave, whatever.

So this book is targeted more at *__how to go about getting better.__* It covers the start-beat-reach-run-finish stuff, but in a different way. It is also about approach, about getting your act together so you can consistently reproduce (and hopefully exceed) your good days.

It is a sad fact of life that often we know what we ought to be doing but habit and inertia leave us settled in our old ways. We carry on doing what we always did and, surprise, surprise, we carry on getting what we always got. As that adage goes: a significant sign of madness is doing the same thing over and over yet expecting a different outcome.

This book, then is a call to action. A call to step outside your comfort zone. To show yourself you can get measurably better at racing around your club cans without spending a fortune, living in the local gym or like a monk.

While improving, you will hopefully also get more fun out of your sailing. And if you feel happier and more fulfilled generally, all well and good – there will be no extra charge!

By all means dip in and out of this book as takes your fancy, but I suggest heeding the distinction between data and information: information is data you actually use to make a difference.

Part 2
Head Faster

Change is the end result of all true learning
Leo Buscaglia

A lot of the high-level sports are really in your mind
Ronald Graham

HOW TO
ACTUALLY GET BETTER

How many self-help books have you read? Did any make a noticeable impact on your life? I hope so, but I doubt it. I want this one actually to have that big impact, for the better and for the long term, not just for next weekend. Which means that, before we get started on the sailing, we need to explore (briefly!) something else: evolution and your brain.

Just like a computer, we have short-term memory (RAM) and long-term memory (disk). This is a good thing – not remembering your partner's name, for example, would be a serious evolutionary mistake. Retaining memory, however, requires energy and your average caveman, just like us, had no need to remember precisely what he had for breakfast three months ago. In fact, it might clutter up his memory and obscure something he did need to know – like where he actually found that breakfast.

The gatekeeper between our short and long-term memory is the hippocampus, which goes back a very long way in evolutionary terms. It is a pretty strict sentry too and very little gets past it – simply reading a book, for example, is unlikely to do the trick. Even worse is that we form very strong habits that can overcome the regular inputs that tell us they are not a good idea - excessive gambling for example. Hence most self-help books fail – the hippocampus prevents the new data from being assimilated properly.

Researchers have identified five steps necessary to get messages past the hippocampus into long-term memory, so overcoming ingrained habits and replacing them with something better. These are:

Pre-contemplation	Before you picked up this book.
Contemplation	Reading this without doing anything else, which will only deliver a fraction of the potential benefit so please do not stop here.
Preparation	Creating an action plan AND committing yourself to seeing it through.
Action	Implementing the plan. The hardest part is consistently repeating the new process until it sticks in long-term memory.

Maintenance   Relapse could be a danger for a long while; it takes effort to keep doing the new, right thing – but look on the bright side, we are not talking about giving up an addiction like smoking.

The good news is that you can boost your Action stage without even leaving the house. Use **visualisation,** an extremely powerful technique used by top sports stars. It is one of the things rugby players are doing when they line up to take a penalty kick.

Consider this experiment in the value of visualisation: in a University of Chicago study, a sample of basketball players was tested for scoring accuracy and then split into three groups. The first group practised getting the ball through the hoop, the second group did nothing extra, and the third used visualisation to imagine themselves scoring cleanly. The 'practised' group improved performance by 24%, the do-nothings got a bit worse, but the visualizers improved by an astonishing 23% without picking up a ball. Amazing, eh?

Another example: when Sally Gunnell won her 400m hurdles Olympic gold medal, she had not only practised for real but she also 'ran' the race in her head a dozen times a day for nine months. If she was not visualising winning (it happens) she stopped and ran it again in her head until she did.

This reminds me of an adage I first heard about musicians; an amateur practises until they get it right, a professional until they cannot get it wrong. With visualisation, you can practise your roll-tacks, gybes, whatever, in the bath, on the train, whenever you get a few moments. Doing so will not only make you better in the boat but also the repetition will help push a new process past your hippocampus. Cool, huh? Just don't start yelling 'Lee-Ho' aloud in the quiet carriage of the 7:35 to London Waterloo.

Final trick, for now. Your brain cannot process a negative (don't think about your sailing hero now – oops, you just did). Always couch key messages in a positive way in your action plan and visualisations. The thought going into a tricky windy day gybe must be 'Stay upright' rather than 'Do not capsize'.

If you truly want to improve your sailing results, commit to using this knowledge and these methods to build and implement your Action Plan.

INPUTS AND OUTPUTS

The wise club sailor will have two critical measures of their own performance. Strangely these are nothing to do with winning.

The first is "How well did I sail?" and the second will be a qualifier: "...in light of the **pre-race** effort I put in". I emphasise the words **pre-race** because once the race has started there is no excuse for not putting in the same level of effort as anyone else - your all.

Let's talk about winning for a moment. I firmly believe winning a race should **not** be your goal. Winning is an outcome but not necessarily a good measure. If winning is the be-all and end-all of your participation in sailing (or in any other sport) then you have my commiserations because, frankly, you may have other psychological issues to deal with.

Why do I say this? If winning is everything, you might choose a class with less competition, or even a club with less competition. You might blow your competitors away with a ridiculous, over-the-top budget, only sail against beginners or rock, pump and generally cheat your way around the course. Or you could just choose a boat solely for its bandit handicap rating. This is not the route to fulfilment, respect from others or even self-respect. If this all sounds like you, stick with us and hopefully we can lead you to a happier place!

The greatest-ever dinghy sailor, Paul Elvstrøm, recognised this issue when he said "You have not won the race if, in winning, you lose the respect of your competitors."

I am sure we have all had days where we were delighted with our own performance – perhaps because we did not capsize on a treacherous day – even if our finishing position was not a five-minute lead over the next boat. Equally, there can be days when you do not feel you sailed as well as you could, but somehow the final placing turned out rather flattering.

Where we need to get to, of course, is the best of both worlds: the satisfaction of a race sailed well and cleanly plus the reward of a good finishing place. Rather like spinning a coin multiple times, the longer the sequence, the more the running outcome will smooth out random factors – and you will get your just desserts.

What we need to do then is minimise the negative impact of our pre-race constraints (or even turn them to our advantage) to raise our standard and consequential race-placings. How best to do that? Below, I've taken some typical constraints and looked at how you can overcome them.

- **Lack of time to sail/practise**
  Make the most of what you have. Cut down the pre- and post-race chit-chat a bit. Launch earlier, practise/sail hard from the moment you launch until the moment you come ashore (i.e. don't meander back and forth for 15 minutes before the start). I bet you could often leave home 20 minutes earlier too. Cut the grass after work one evening, rather than leaving it until the weekend.

- **Low budget, old boat, tired sails**
  Love your ship regardless. Give it a polish. Lubricate the fittings. Make sure it is still set up properly so nothing will break. Do a deal with a fleet hotshot for a set of his retired sails.

  Former National Champion Keith Videlo used to whop us all in a Laser with the most clapped-out, stretched, porous sail you ever saw, a daggerboard that looked like a shark had tried it for lunch and a hull covered in algae.

  Remember that when you get ahead of someone who is in a brand-new ship, they will be **so** frustrated at themselves.

- **Lack of fitness**
  Given the choice, an hour on the water is preferable to an hour in the gym. No pain-no gain. Just go for it, push yourself and improved fitness will come.

  Padded hiking shorts are a revelation in some boat designs; suddenly sitting out is not so bad after all. If your gunwales dig into your legs, a pair of hikers may be the best sailing present you ever get.

- **Increasing age**
  Paul Elvstrøm sailed a Tornado at the Seoul Olympics at the age of 60 and did not embarrass himself. Age truly is an attitude – ignore your kids' leg-pulling, what do they know?

  Running for President of the USA in 1984 at the age of 73, against an opponent 20 years' younger, Ronald Reagan said, "I want you to know that I will not make age an issue of this campaign. I am not going to exploit, for political purposes, my opponent's youth and inexperience". Of course, he did just that, and so should you.

- **Inexperience**
…equals more open to learning and fewer entrenched bad habits. Get out there at every opportunity, rain or shine. Ask your fleet captain to assign you a *buddy*. Ask questions (but please not the same one five times). Soak up the knowledge and love climbing that learning curve.

- **Too light/heavy/tall/short**
Learn how to make your rig work for your specific circumstances; after all, they are called tuning **guides** (not **requirements**)

  Some top light-air specialists have been heavyweights themselves and vice-versa. Weight mostly makes a (marginal) difference in marginal conditions. Be positive and turn it into a strength.

  Some realism won't hurt either. Have a look at the section on choosing the right boat. If you are five-foot tall and seven stone in your hobnailed-boots then neither a Phantom nor a Finn is the right boat for you. Sorry.

Journalist sports commentators (as opposed to sporting-stars retired to the media) often talk about 'will to win'. Utter nonsense mostly. Hating to lose, refusing to be beaten are negative emotions and far more powerful (and common) drivers. When you're having a ding-dong with someone up the final beat, do you tend to think "I'll be so happy if I finish in front of you" or "No way I am letting you beat me sunshine"?

Budget
We have all felt intimidated occasionally by the 'throw loadsa money at it' brigade. And yes, unconstrained budget can help.

But hang on – what's the objective here? Surely it is to have fun. I bet someone on a tight (or no) budget has far more fun per pound spent than Mr Flash-the-Cash. Some big spenders certainly get upset when things do not go their way!

Do be sensible, though, about your choice of boat. Of course you will not win the International 14 Prince of Wales Cup with a £2,000 boat, but you can have lots of thrills and some great racing.

Crew

Unless you sail single-handed, you need them. Probably more than they need you. So be good to them. Always. When I heap praise on my son for, say, a great kiwi (a right on the mark gybe-kite-drop) he replies, "Of course it was. I did it." Let it ride – and do not ever rant when something goes wrong – that only makes things worse.

DOING WHAT YOU KNOW YOU SHOULD

Is this the definition of a club sailor: someone who knows what they ought to do, but does not actually do it? Chances are, you have read lots of books and know what ought to be happening with your boat but that wisdom is not actually crossing the divide from theory to practice.

Which means the problem is actually in your head. It is all about attitude and approach. If we are going to get you further up the fleet, these have to be changed. Frankly, you are in a rut, whether you realise it or not. We need to break some habits and build a new routine.

Try visualising your next race day with these actions slotted in;

1. Sit down and eat a sensible **breakfast** before you leave. I'm not proposing a special Redgrave and Pinsent carb-fest. Just fry an egg or heat some baked beans and whack them on a slice or two of toast. A bar of anything that comes in a wrapper does not qualify here.

2. And have an extra **drink** – doesn't matter what, just take in more fluid than usual.

3. Take a water **bottle** with you – keep the levels topped up.

4. Before you leave home, log on to the Internet and check the **weather**. The BBC /Met Office are useless in my opinion – I find windfinder.com and XCweather.co.uk the least worst, while Metcheck tries to give probabilities and some people like Windguru. Many clubs have a real-time weather station and/or webcams relayed on their website. If that facility is available, use it.

5. If applicable, also check the **tide** times. If you will not remember the high/low water times, write them on the back of your hand or arm.

6. On the way to the sailing club, turn the car stereo off for a couple of minutes and think about how the forecast wind (strength and direction) and tide are likely to affect your particular stretch of water and so **shape your race**(s).

7. If your route (or a quick detour) allows you to view the sailing water, do it. Park up if you can safely. Look and **appraise** how conditions compare against the forecast, in wind strength, direction and sea

state. If these conflict with the forecast, have a ponder why that might be and what might happen next, and when.

8. If you can't stop on the way, *appraise* on arrival.

9. Now start thinking about your *strategy* for the race. Areas of wind shadow, wind bends, tidal eddies and strongest flow. Visualise the snakes and ladders of the race course, how you can use the ladders and, particularly, avoid the snakes.

10. Only when you have done these, get *rigged and changed* etc. Need it or not, have a pee now whilst it is not too inconvenient.

11. Do not forego the pre-race banter; that's all part of the fun after all, but have a sense of purpose and a *spring in your step*. You are going sailing, wahoo, not grinding away in the office, vacuuming or cutting the grass.

12. Jog down to the boat, have a *stretch* of the muscles that will be working hard later. Smile at the likely sarcastic comments – after all, you know something today that they do not!

13. Try and launch a couple of minutes earlier than usual. As soon as you are off, go *straight into race mode*. On arrival at the start/course area, stand up, have a look about and consider your strategic thoughts from earlier – do they still apply or do they need adapting? Invert your thinking about the snakes though; instead, positively visualise the places you will go. It is a strange truism that if you focus on a hole in the road, you will hit it as if magnetically drawn, so shift your focus to where you positively want to be.

14. Whilst standing, have another stretch and a shadow-box to get the *adrenaline* going. In my 470 days, we used to have a muck-about mock wrestle that was hilarious. Someone will no doubt take the mickey again. Plan your response to the hecklers in advance - a smug smile or Paddington Bear stare is cool if you can carry it off.

15. Do not just reach back and forth awaiting the start. Keep lining up starts at each end and *assessing* the wind angle and bias. This should give you a real feel for the size and frequency of the windshifts and gusts.

16. Also hoist the *kite* and check it is rigged properly. Gybe it and

recheck. Better to find out now than be embarrassed later. Murphy's Law says that the day you get to the windward mark first without checking it will be the day you discover it is rigged sideways. I suggest this is not the sort of award you should be shooting for.

17. Have another drink. **Check** foils for weed. If your control lines migrate from one side to another during a race, shift them the other way in anticipation.

18. **Start plan**. Lots of textbooks focus on starting at the favoured end. More important is to be sailing in clear air on the correct tack asap. Starting at the port end can leave you pinned on the headed tack for ages. Generally that is not a good thing; being out-of-phase is often far more costly than the gain from a bit of line bias.

19. Work out where you want the control lines set for the first leg. This may involve lots of kicker and cunningham but, if they are maxed on during pre-start jockeying, you will struggle to manoeuvre or stop when you need to. Instead, **squeeze** them on as you are 'pulling the trigger' in the final few seconds. A great job for a crew to take on.

20. Even if you do not normally, today you are going to get in there and mix it up a bit at the start. Pole position is not the ultimate objective for now. Visualise building speed up pre-start so you are in the **front rank 20 seconds after the gun**. Of course, many club-race starts are from a fixed line and sometimes the first leg is downwind. We will cover such eventualities later but for now the key, the absolute priority, is to avoid the fleet sucking you into the snake-zone.

OK. In a moment I want you to stop reading, close your eyes and imagine your next sailing day with as many of these 20 points as you can remember slotted into it. Go on. Close your eyes and visualise…

Welcome back. Feel like the outcome of that race might be better than usual? Even though I bet you could only remember a few of the points in the list.

To make it all come true, keep re-reading and visualising until all 20 come to mind effortlessly. To help you, I have put the action-clues in bold italics for each point. The objective is to get to the state where this is your *unthinking* routine. A checklist is **not** the right way here. You do not need a checklist for getting up and out of the house on a workday. We need this process to become second nature in the same way – it has to get past that hippocampus.

RELENTLESSNESS

I have been lucky enough at my club to sail against some of the UK's best amateur sailors, particularly Keith Videlo, Nick Craig and Roger Gilbert. Even in a club race, their focus, intensity and relentlessness still eclipse anyone else's. What is more, they are all lovely guys.

Their starts are sublime; they are not only always on the right shift but perfectly positioned for the next one; their boat handling is immaculate, flatter than you can imagine; their boats seem to keep moving when everyone else's slow or stop in lulls; they hike longer and harder. No matter how windy it is, capsizes never seem to happen. They keep all this going for every second until the finish.

What I find interesting is how, sometimes, some more ordinary mortals manage to hang on in there with them for a while. But as the race goes on, mistakes creep in and they fade away from the front in the onslaught of the champs' relentlessness.

What then, apart from the obvious (no mistakes) is the lesson for the rest of us?

Being relentless is far easier said than done. These guys have practised long, hard and effectively. They are fit and strong and have the confidence to know they are likely to prevail if they keep it up. But we are club sailors; this is not about beating 100-plus others at a Nationals or Worlds. It is a club race. The rest of us can still apply the 'relentless' principle. If you can do it more effectively than the others do, you too are more likely to prevail. If the others up their game too, the battle will still be far more satisfying than just wallowing around daydreaming.

How do you do this? Some of my earlier tips about eating and drinking should enhance your ability to raise your performance level. The following chapter about The Inner Game will help you on the straight and narrow too.

Even more important, though, is to recognise and embrace the issue - to be relentless too. Avoid weasel compromises with yourself - "That's flat enough", "I know it is a header really but I'm sure it will back even more in a minute", "Banging the corner really is the right thing to do". Please, please stop kidding yourself. Relentless claptrap is not what we need.

Another element of relentlessness concerns your mood and emotions. Emotions are important; without them we would be robots. In a racing boat, however, they tend to get in the way. So if a surge of adrenalin following a mistake makes you hike like a superstar and retrieve yourself, run with it if you are in a simple drag race. But don't lose sight of the bigger picture. There is no point blowing another boat away in raw anger if 10 simply sail around you both. Stay analytical and keep the priorities balanced.

I'd therefore like to propose a little *relentlessness* self-test question that you can and should use, perhaps every minute or less: "In this situation, what would *<insert name of your sailing hero here>* do now?" Then do that, without hesitation or equivocation. If the answer is a vague "Not have put themselves here" perhaps you need to ask yourself this question even more often and act upon the answers.

THE INNER GAME OF TENNIS

(… or sailing or anything else)

If you have not read Timothy Galwey's classic book, I strongly recommend you do so. It is easy to read, refreshingly short and still in print 50 years on. Applying the principles to sailing instead of tennis is straightforward – these are universal truths and wise words. Meantime, I shall paraphrase.

Galwey's underlying principle is 'muscle-memory'. There are many processes our bodies deal with that require no conscious thought: breathing, eating, even picking something up. Your body knows what to do without a stream of detailed instructions from your inner voice. Further, humans have an ability to mimic a physical action far more effectively than relying on vocalised instructions. To test that, get a friend to try stroking their chin three times with their ring finger solely by obeying physical movement instructions you give them. No describing the target or objective – just left, right, up, down and with what.

Tricky, isn't it?

Now say "Do this" and touch your left earlobe with the little finger of your right hand. I suspect that worked rather better. Quicker too.

Galwey worked out that this principle also applies to, say, a topspin backhand. When in mimic mode, feet almost automatically go to the right place and arm movements work well. Past difficulties with the shot melt away.

In times of stress and pressure, though, our conscious mind decides it knows better than our muscle memory – and starts to butt in. Our brain then starts dishing out detailed instructions, confusing, drowning out or contradicting our muscle memory. But what does Mr Brain know? **He's** never gybed at a mark surrounded by upturned boats. True, he was a passenger when your body did it all those other times, but when was it ever a good idea to let a passenger land a jumbo jet?

So let us analyse when this syndrome tends to kick in. When there is an important gybe coming up. When someone we want to impress is watching. When we are about to win a certain type of race or event or even just beat Joe Bloggs for the first time ever. Then, Mr Brain sticks his oar in. We start 'thinking' about it. Boatspeed flies out of the window as we tense up. Gybes turn to swims, tacks go all wrong, Joe B gets closer and closer. Stress levels increase further. More things go wrong. Next thing we know, we have grabbed defeat from the jaws of victory. Doh!

What is the solution? Well, first we need to understand the issue. Next we need to get Mr Brain to stick with his own job. What he can do usefully for us is gather and process some information. What is the safest route through that graveyard of upturned hulls? What is the wind doing? Where is the pressure? Where should we position the boat to cover the opposition? Is the rig set up right for the conditions? Which is the favoured end of the finish line? Alternatively you can just tell him to shut up and sing you an appropriate song – preferably neither "Another one bites the dust" nor "We are the champions" until you cross the line *and* hear a finish signal.

Manage all of this and perhaps we can banish the curse of choking. Easier said than done, of course – it is the primary redeeming factor in ever watching golfists on TV – the human drama that is the external manifestation of The Inner Game.

LUCK

Is it true some people are naturally lucky and others magnets for misfortune?

Gary Player, the golfer, famously said that the more he practised, the luckier he got. In his long rivalry with Arnold Palmer, both felt the other got all the lucky breaks whenever they came out second-best. This is an egocentric self-delusion we all have. If things go well, it is a result of our skills, effort, talent and charm, but if they go badly, that outcome is all down to injustice and the excessive, unfair good fortune of others.

Both conclusions are nonsense, of course. Everyone else out there is trying too, has their own strengths and weaknesses and manages risks and opportunities in their own way. Thankfully this usually gives rise to some predictable and some surprising results - imagine how dull and pointless things would be otherwise. So embrace the contrasts and variations in a positive way. Research shows that optimists, positive thinkers get more from life (are luckier) than pessimists.

How can this be? The answer is about awareness and receptivity. The pessimist bemoans, say, the shifty conditions when they get a couple wrong. The optimist sees those same shifts providing plenty of opportunity to make up lost ground and perhaps even feeds off others' clear frustration converting it to positive energy and so benefit.

In his book The Luck Factor, following 10 years of research, Prof Richard Wiseman identifies four principles to create your own good fortune:

1. **Maximise Chance Opportunities**
   Such as being in the middle rather than banging the corners.

2. **Listen to Lucky Hunches**
   Ever had that, "I knew I should have…" feeling? Experience and subconscious knowledge often tell us something we cannot rationalise and vocalise. Perhaps your brain is not just pulling ideas out of nothing after all.

3. **Expect Good Fortune**
   Stuff happens. You will have lucky as well as unlucky breaks. When you get a lucky lift, up the beat and be ready to use it to your best ends – perhaps sailing low and fast to crystallise the gain over the bunch rather than hanging high and losing out again on the next header.

4. **Turn Bad Luck to Good**
   Things could have been worse. You could have crashed the car on the way to sail. You could be at home doing <*insert most hated chore here*>. You could have been on the starboard layline when the big left shift came. Take control and do not dwell on negatives. You now know big shifts are happening, so what will the next one be?

Prof Wiseman now runs a Luck School – is that lucky or what? So, are you a lucky person who will take the hint and explore this avenue further OR an unlucky one who will skip over such a steer? The latter group will never know what they have missed of course.

(Bad) luck should also be considered in the context of attention-seeking behaviour. In business would you rather employ the 'trouble shooter' who is adept at conjuring new ways for innovative disasters to happen, then (mostly) fixing them OR the serene types for whom everything is in order and nothing seems to go wrong? I choose the latter; I'll get my excitement elsewhere thanks. Back to boats, if you sail with someone in this former category, my advice is to get out of there as fast as you can. Stay friends, enjoy their stories at the bar but find someone else to sail with. The day you do that will become one of your luckier days!

ARE YOU IN THE RIGHT BOAT?

What we sail is inevitably a compromise. We have to balance a range of factors: ability, budget, crew availability, club-approved classes, sailing water constraints, weight, height, agility, age and fitness among others.

Confession: I am a firm believer that class racing gives rise to a strong sailing club whilst menagerie racing represents a slippery and dangerous slope. Yet at the time of writing I club-sail my RS100, the only one at my club. In my defence, I do tour with the 100 and also club-race my Laser. Nevertheless, my hypocrisy is exposed.

More than anything else, I would still suggest the first choice should be a class sailed actively at your local club. If none of them suits you, what about another nearby club?

My hypocrisy also extends to the fact that I sail single-handers while believing that two-handers are actually better for clubs in the long run. Sadly, having once (no longer, obviously) been a pretty decent crew, I suffer from a pathetic syndrome whereby I am fairly confident that no crew with abilities matching my expectations would lower themselves to crew for me. Not for long anyway.

While there is lots of information available about individual classes and the boats mentioned below are indicative ideas not recommendations, to help you make a sensible decision about what to sail, I recommend you work through the following list of questions,:

- **Single or two-hander**
  Take care sailing with your partner. If doing so creates stress, is there another boat in the fleet in the same situation - if so the answer is obvious.
- **Body weight**
  If you are 5' 2" tall and weigh 8 stone, sorry, but a Finn is not the answer for you. Ben can rest easy. An International Moth, 420 or 470 will do nicely though, to name but three.
- **Skill level**
  If you are still struggling to master the club training boats, you should probably leave it a while before leaping onto a 49er, Moth or Musto Skiff.
- **Tight racing or extreme performance**
  As a generalisation, the less extreme the boat the physically closer the racing – even if only because five seconds in a 49er takes you much

further than five seconds in a Mirror. I love the nip-and-tuck of Laser racing but we all love going seriously fast too – just remember it is largely the *impression* of speed that counts, so do not discount the more traditional classes.

- **Travel or club only**
  If you want to hit the circuit but the nearest open is 400 miles away, perhaps it is time for something else...

- **SMOD, one-design or development class**
  Like boat bimbling or actual sailing? Is out-engineering the completion part of the game for you or an expensive irrelevance? Personally, I like the mano-a-mano, no excuses game that comes from one-designs, particularly a SMOD but each to their own.

- **Financial budget**
  Be realistic. Please do not buy a disintegrating pile of junk because it feels glam. It will almost certainly let you down, particularly when you come up against a decent model. Be warned, you are unlikely to sail it as much as you imagined before you signed the cheque.

- **Menagerie or class racing**
  Was it our refusal to be satisfied that put the Great in Great Britain? Is sailing now the only place left where that principle still applies? Perhaps. We seem to have more classes than anywhere else, while so many countries appear to sail what the ISAF tells them to (i.e. International Classes). We Brits tend to be contrary – 14,000 plus Fireballs, under 1,000 470s; the French 470 numbers seem to parallel the UK Fireball numbers. Not hard to guess which was invented where!

  Ah, the agony of choice. Try out the most popular classes at your local clubs. Unless there is a good reason not to, (budget, size etc) go with the best of those. It is worth looking at circuit dates too though, a couple of local opens can add some welcome spice to life.

In all of this, do not forget it is about the camaraderie too. There's no point buying a boat you love if you cannot stand the people who sail them (unlikely, but it can happen) or the way they race (too intense, too laid back).

If in doubt, takes lots of counsel. Look at the For Sale boards (class associations, Apollo Duck and Yachts & Yachting are good starters). Lacking confidence? Ask your fleet captain what to look out for. Take someone you trust along with you if you are uncertain.

And always remember to assess how easy the thing will be to sell later on, when you are ready to try something else or upgrade. It is always easy to buy a boat; not necessarily so easy to sell it on.

CLOTHING

Has anyone else noticed that many sailing club changing-rooms seem to be too small nowadays, even though turnouts are often not what they used to be? I have a theory: it isn't that the changing-rooms are too small – it's that our kitbags are now too big.

Back in my student days, we thought nothing of sailing in jeans all winter, or perhaps in a homemade two-piece wetsuit. They were truly awful. On windy days, we would put on a couple of extra Arran jumpers – not for warmth but as surrogate weight jackets. Crazy.

Later, I first encountered the agony of too much choice. Launching the 470 off the beach for Weymouth Olympic Week, the Finn guys were a great source of entertainment. Whatever the weather, a huge kitbag would be emptied into the boat and they would launch wearing just a pair of swimming briefs. Then they would sail off, wriggling into a shorty, say. They'd have a little 'test-it' sail. Then shrug. Then it was off with the shorty and on with something else. This pantomime could continue for hours. I never did work out where they put the rejected stuff during the race.

The upside of that is the great kit that is now available – hot or cool base layers, really comfortable wetsuits, warm, breathable outer layers, drysuits that do not act as a personal sauna and padded hiking shorts that dispel the agony of un-ergonomic topsides. As Billy Connolly quotes his fishing friend saying, "There is no such thing as bad weather, just the wrong clothes". As a result, I often think I prefer racing in the winter to the summer. Nowadays, I confess to the luxury of a Saturday set and a Sunday set so that when I do go away for a weekend there is none of that wet-wetsuit unpleasantness on the second day. No wonder kitbags now come with wheels.

If you're still sailing in discarded gardening clothes, hand-me-downs or smelly mementos from 20 years ago, do yourself a favour. Head for the chandlers, pick their brains, try on lots of stuff and either splash the cash or make a Christmas/birthday wish list. You will not regret it. But you might need a bigger kitbag.

Will all this new kit make you sail faster? If gunwale edges hurt your legs, then definitely – hiking shorts are a wonder. If you suffer from cold, then definitely. If your buoyancy aid is a 30 year-old vest lacking bubbles, you might be saving your own bacon.

WHAT LEVEL OF SAILOR ARE YOU?

I have a working theory that there are four progressive 'modes' of sailing, being

1. Flolloping along, not really bothered about how well the boat is sailed, but at least you are on the water.

2. Trying to work out how to sail the boat properly and fast.

3. You have broadly worked out how: the challenge is putting theory into practice.

4. You sail the boat without really thinking about it; the effort is in the strategy, tactics and squeezing out that ultimate extra drop of speed.

As you are reading this, you have evolved past level 1 – which is good news as staying at that level is fine and dandy but also represents a missed opportunity to get so much more from your sailing.

Conversely, the video of the Beijing Olympics 49er medal race is proof, if it were needed, that even the top sailors are not always at level 4. It was great entertainment. Boats were capsizing all over the place, a couple within yards of finishing to secure gold. The (Danish) eventual Gold winners had been four seconds short of five minutes late for the start, having broken their mast, gone in, rigged a borrowed boat and sailed back out again. They needed to be in seventh place to win – and they were, when they too fell in yards from the line, but righted and just finished without losing another place.

While we all shuffle between various levels depending on circumstances and conditions, there are huge gains to be made from raising your game up a level. Lots of self-help books are aimed at those on level 1 and even more on honing you at level 4, but most of us are somewhere in the middle.

Knowing where you are on this scale in any situation can be really helpful in deciding what your priority should be at any moment.

FOR RELATIVE BEGINNERS

If this sailboat racing business is new to you, it is easy to psyche yourself out knowing other racers are more experienced. Do not fall into this trap! The old lags hardly ever practise, tend to be stuck in a rut and rarely analyse their performance. So a bit of determination and effort can put you on a fast track past them if you are willing to go for it.

Here are a few pointers to focus on:

- Relative beginners have not had time to develop their 'automatic pilot' – the ability to sail at 80% efficiency or more when not concentrating fully on the driving. Be aware of this risk: do not find yourself sailing 30 degrees off the wind on a beat. Time on the water is the ultimate solution. If you sail a two-hander, either delegate a distracting task to the crew or make them watch the jib tell-tales and nudge you if they stop streaming properly while your attention is elsewhere.

- Try to imagine how events are going to unfold around you. If you are unsure where another boat is headed (it may be on a different leg, or even in a different race) do not be too shy to open a conversation. Shouting "starboard" isn't the only approach. Saying "I'll go behind you" can save lots of hassle for both boats. Similarly, if someone slightly to windward has a spinnaker up on a gusty day, expect them to lose control and sail at you. If the worst happens, never mind the rules. Avoid them anyway, with a smile and sympathetic word, thereby making a friend – and collect a beer later.

- Commit to going for it. A very common hurdle for starting-racers is what I call 'slow-bicycles syndrome'. This is where they do not sit out hard enough, only partly sheet in, then panic when a gust hits and heels the boat. In panic they over-compensate, let the sheet go then have to jump into the boat in panic as it heels to windward. The boom swings wildly at them, the boat screws up beyond close-hauled and a sore head may well ensue.

  Understandably, this feels wobbly, frightening and frankly dangerous. Compare it with riding a bike, where speed brings stability, or driving a car where we can balance throttle and clutch readily enough to perform a hill start. The boat is no different. Commit. Get the weight over the side, power on with the sheet and play it to keep things balanced. Later we will talk about the sail controls for managing power delivery, after which you can make sure you are, metaphorically, hill-starting in first gear not fifth.

Another potential impediment to relative beginners: the old buffers who have been sailing around the same water for decades. Lacking any perspective, they now believe they own the water and that their multi-decade rivalry with old Harry for eighth place of 10 makes the Olympics pale into irrelevance. Anyone unfortunate enough to 'get in my way' is likely to receive a serious tongue-lashing. Of course they would never dare censure better and more experienced sailors ahead of them in the same way. There is a word for this: bullying. It is covered in the Racing Rules of Sailing. If you ever experience or witness this intolerable behaviour, do something about it; it must be stopped. Talk to your Fleet Captain, Sailing Secretary, a Flag Officer or the Treasurer (we bean-counters hate the thought of losing income!) That should get it fixed. If not, frankly that club needs naming and shaming too.

Thankfully, probably the biggest challenge is the actual sailing. We dedicated, sad fanatics have been out there trying hard for ages and the gap between front and back can *feel* seriously insurmountable. Stick with it. It *is* possible to succeed, even if you are a relatively late starter. Read this book, ask for help, set yourself some goals. Have a look around the boat park at the competition. Most of us do not exactly have the honed physique of sporting gods, do we? Truly, if we can do it, so can you. So please persevere and do not be put off by the first tricky day or inevitable swim.

FOR TEENAGERS

My ambition for you as a young sailor is probably different: for you to enjoy some form of sailing throughout your life – and to be as keen to sail as my friend and hero Charlie. In his ninth decade, he still sails his Solo and those two artificial hips are certainly not going to stop him.

The good news is that the choice of classes, the boats themselves, equipment and clothing are so much better than back in my youth. It is also possible to make a career out of sailing in way it never was before. The bad news is that we live in a world obsessed with Health & Safety that seeks to exclude you from much of the mischief and cowboy behaviour we got away with. Then there are the ubiquitous pressures of seemingly perpetual exams.

If those were not enough, sailing now how has an extremely effective coaching structure. Is it too much like going to school though? Is this why so many give up?

Personally, I am not a great lover of this coaching structure as it stands. Indisputably, it is extremely efficient at building a medal winning GBR team. Hooray! But does anyone tell you that there is life (and perhaps far more partying and fun) outside the five-ring circus tent? Does anyone tell you that your chances of getting in the team are perhaps worse than one in ten thousand*? My concern is that it is easy to embark on the Zone Squad trail but too little emphasis is given to ensuring a comfortable exit when the time inevitably comes. This is not good for you and not good for the sport of sailing in general. Too many leave the squads put off sailing for ever.

It need not be this way. Now forewarned, you are forearmed. You can now manage things on your terms, not theirs. Refuse to let them spoil your fun. The way I suggest you do so is this:

1. **Increase your repertoire**
    Sail everything you can. Single-handers, double-handers, boats with symmetric, asymmetric or no kite at all. Monohulls and cats. Have a go at trapezing. Sail the ultra-trendy but try a GP14 and appeciate its virtues too. Crew for anyone, star or muppet. Try a sailboard and keelboat. Find out what you enjoy most, something that will truly light your fire. You don't necessarily know what it is yet but if you don't explore the options you never will.

*this number was established by extremely thorough and
diligent guessing, but you get the idea*

2. **Do something outside the Zone Squads**

   Sail the RS200, Lark or Fireball nationals. Try the Southport 24 hour race. Try team-racing and get to some tournaments. Talk to squad-escapees who are still sailing and discover how much more joy their sailing now brings them.

3. **Manage your parents**

   They will have given up a huge amount of time and money, perhaps sacrificing their own sailing for you. Respect their effort and remember that they love you – particularly when it feels like they are giving you a hard time (which is far less fun for them than it is for you).

   Talk to them about your sailing goals, discuss what is realistically achievable and agree how you will deal with both set-backs and successes. Agree your plan for dismounting the Zone Squad escalator and what you will do thereafter.

4. **Be independent**

   Agree a plan with your parents for passing your driving test before your 18th birthday. Do not assume this means you get the family car to drive! Start thinking about how you will earn, at the minimum, some beer and boat-fittings money.

Above all, remember that sailing is fun. That is why we do it. It is the ultimate sport and we love it. Do not let 'the establishment' put you off. It is your life. Refuse to let them spoil sailing for you.

FOR THE CREW

This section is written for the crew only. If you are the helm, please stop reading at this point and pass the book over to your crew to read. Thank you.

OK crew. Have they gone? Are we alone? Don't read this where they can see you! Find somewhere private, because laughing out loud and pointing at your helm in the next few minutes might spoil your relationship.

Right, here are some things that you already know deep down - but they need independent affirmation. Your unspoken thoughts are perfectly normal. Yes, helms really are complete numpties. They take on too much. They delegate and share too little. They assume the crew is the weakest link. They fall over at vital moments or drop the tiller or sheet. They tack or gybe without telling you. They make mutually exclusive commands. They squat casually on the side while demanding you straight-leg hike with only your knees downwards in the boat. They demand information then shoot the messenger if the news is bad. After the race, they will blame you for something minor or even imagined while their own bloopers are glossed over. In the event of victory, guess who takes all the plaudits. Don't you just love the 'the nut on the tiller'?

In their defence, most of them pay the bills, spend hours maintaining the boat and do the organising. Some might buy the tea between races or even the snifter when the sun crosses the yardarm. So they do have their uses. The key thing to remember is that they are doing their best, bless them. Give them their due, they probably even found you this to read, so they are trying, in their own special way.

With any luck, they have now, finally, worked out that you are a valuable resource, not just moveable ballast with hands attached. Which means they are receptive to change. The time for you to emerge from the shadows is upon us.

So what can you do? Firstly, say to them "Can I borrow this book please?" then read and digest. Step two: have a frank chat about goals, ('a laugh' is just as acceptable target as coming third or whatever in the series) inputs, commitment and constraints. Hopefully you will achieve a meeting of minds and a new sense of purpose and direction. You might even decide to step up to something more exciting or challenging to sail.

The next step is to agree who will do what, in and out of the boat. More responsibility or even just input from you will equal more enjoyment and better results. For example, chatting through the strategy for the day's conditions will always lead to a better plan – as Zaphod Beeblebrox* concluded, two heads truly are better than one. So you too should read the weather forecast and know the tide-times.

Your greatest contribution is in the boat, though. Things like:

1. Balance. When the boat is overpowered, hike like your life depends on it. Look at the position of the boom to see if the helm has eased it to shed power and keep the boat flat. If so, now is not the time for a rest. In light airs, your role in balance terms is to let the helm be comfortable; you are the course adjustment, allowing their small movements to be the difference that keeps the boat flat.

2. Upwind, closely observe the slot between jib and mainsail, particularly towards the top (spreaders provide a useful reference point). That slot is paramount. Too wide means speed wasted. Too narrow is referred to as 'choked' for good reason. Cherish that slot as you might your own child. See the section on sail trim for more.

3. If you don't already, start handling the sail control lines (kicker and cunningham). Develop a feel for how far to pull them, look up and observe the impact on the sail shape. Be ready to give them a bit extra in the gusts and ease in the lulls.

4. Accept that what appear to be seats in the boat are not there for sitting on. Your weight needs to be positioned optimally fore and aft. Murphy's Law dictates that this will be uncomfortable. Sorry.

5. Watch for other boats, not just to avoid collisions but also to anticipate clear wind lanes. Share this information. It is seriously annoying to miss opportunity to tack on a nice shift because of seen but not mentioned traffic.

6. Look out for the darkened water that is an approaching gust. Count the gust in aloud. At the beginning, your timing is likely to be out, but you will improve over time. Move in anticipation. A bit of windward heel in anticipation of the gust is fast. The same principles apply to lulls.

*If you haven't read *The Hitchhikers Guide to the Galaxy*, it's time you did. It's unlikely to make you sail faster but is a wonderful book nevertheless

7. Don't wait to be asked, on white sail reaches, play the jib continuously so that all six tell-tales are always streaming perfectly. This may require moving the jib leads forward or acting as a human fairlead (when you can reach) because jibs often twist too much when the sheets are eased.

8. When the kite is up, never ever take your eye off the thing. Play it constantly. Keep providing feedback: how the sheet-load feels (strong or soft and floppy), whether the pole has had to come too far back or an asymmetric is flopping at the leech (or vice versa). This is invaluable to help the helm know whether they need to come up or can bank some profit bearing off.

9. Be indefatigable. Never give up or let spirits sink. Helms are fragile creatures. Look after their delicate egos. Keep them happy and amused. The last thing you want is a helm that feels guilty that they are letting you down. They are moody enough as it is!

10. Be realistic. Stuff will go wrong. It's not actually easy back there. If it was easy, it would be boring.

11. Non-judgemental feedback please. Be objective in your observations but not critical. Couch bad news with a useful contribution. "Joe Bloggs is faster than us" may be factually correct but is not good for morale. "Joe Bloggs is sitting a bit further aft and sailing lower but making less leeway. Looks sweet" is much better.

12. Do your fair share off the water. Help rig and unrig, particularly when it's cold or pouring down.

The best way to appreciate the challenges someone else faces is of course to swap roles. Persuade them to let you have a go at the back. Just don't get hooked on the authority and control!

Part 3
Around the Course

Action expresses priorities
Mohandas Gandhi

Good things happen when you get your priorities straight
Scott Caan

TACTICS

The key here is to have a firm grasp of the priorities and stick to them. Those priorities, however, will change according to where you are sailing and the conditions on the day. The key aspects to consider are:

- **Wind speed**
  In ghosting conditions, wind speed is everything. Finding 2 knots when the competition is in half a knot or less could see you travelling several times faster.
  Being in greater pressure pays most of the way up the scale, getting you moving faster or even planing when others are not.
  At some point though, the tables will turn and we have more than enough to wind handle – any more just adds to drag from the rig and risks going for a swim. Just occasionally, then, shelter is handy.
- **Tide/current**
  In some situations tide is everything but whenever a tangible current is present it will have some impact. Do not forget that current can also have an impact on sea state. A wind against tide chop can be a real impediment to keeping the boat moving.
- **Geographical features**
  Nearby land can have all sorts of impacts, such as:
    - Wind bends, whether caused by the airflow being guided around a corner or sheered as it crosses a shoreline.
    - Windshifts. Wind blowing off the land is invariably shiftier and less predictable.
    - Pressure bands and funnels – the cliffs at Lake Garda being the legendary example. If you ever have the chance to try Garda, grab it.
    - Wind shadows can be present on both lee and weather shores – watch out for downdrafts too.
    - Sea state. Headlands, islands and the like can have an impact on any chop or waves. You might want to avoid them, they might become your friends.
- **Weather**
  Whether short-term (a big black cloud) or longer-term (a weather front, a sea-breeze) the impact could be big gains or big losses. Remember that if the weather changes significantly, you will need to revisit other aspects of your plan too. I am not advocating that you become a meteorologist, just that you are awake to the possibility of something changing.

- **Course**
  At a championship, there is a good chance you will be on open water with a straightforward, well-laid course of triangles, sausages and the like. Uniform may well be the best description. Club sailing is a completely different matter. With marks scattered all over the place and perhaps fixed (running?) start-lines things are in many ways more complex. Start-lines and beats can be biased and knowledge of local quirks paramount. As an example, take Chichester Harbour Fed Week where at least four interacting tidal streams need to be managed, never mind trying to work out which mark is which.

Inevitably, all of those factors present will interact. Do some planning to establish the priorities and stick to your game plan. At all costs, avoid being derailed by other boats. For example, blast low to re-establish a clear wind lane if someone tacks on you. Sometimes you may even have to grin and bear it if the alternative is worse (like tacking into an adverse current).

Map out your plan for the race duration and take into account that what may be best at the time of the start may not be two laps later when the tide has changed.

As club sailors, our infallibility is not necessarily guaranteed. If your best judgement is trumped by someone else's it *may* be time to amend your plan. Bear in mind they might just have struck lucky. Try to analyse *why* it worked out for them and then recast your thinking in light of this new information. If you are in a two-hander, use the available help. Get the crew to watch for unexpected developments and boats making extraordinary gains and losses. Talk through the tactical situation together – that process itself should help clarify the thinking.

Never give up mentally or descend to sailing around randomly with your mind in neutral. Keep trying, keep analysing and testing your hypotheses: it could all come good yet. If not, after the race you can ask the winner how they did it, what their edge was. That way, even if your result is not what you hoped for today, you will have learned something useful for next time.

STARTS

Downwind starts

We club-racers sometimes experience a delight you do not encounter on the Olympic Circuit – ah, the challenges and delights of a downwind start and the first mark chaos that invariably follows.

The goal for the start and first leg is simply to get yourself into pole position for the first mark rounding. Get yourself on the inside and you are laughing. But if you have to give water (oops – 'room') to the whole fleet, you could be on the outside of a very large cartwheel and lose an eon.

How do you make that break and get clear ahead? A fast start usually helps. That means hitting the line at full speed as the gun goes – this may give you those two or three lengths needed to avoid being swallowed by the bunch behind. Your next priority is clear wind, whatever it takes – get low in the gusts, heat it up in the lulls, look for the gaps in the bunch that the wind will accelerate through, have a gentle word with the neighbours to persuade them to race the fleet and not just you (so you can break together), then apply the five essentials perfectly with whatever breeze you have.

Sometimes, though, even these are not enough and you will find yourself in the bunch. Do not despair; you can still apply the same principles, but overlaid with the objective of positioning your boat for the mark-rounding chaos to come – if you start planning early you will likely be in a minority, sometimes a minority of one. You need to work yourself to the side of the fleet that puts you on the inside track. If you are boxed in by a large gaggle of boats and you will struggle to get clear ahead of them in time, slow down a bit now so you can manoeuvre, perhaps even gybe off to get out of there. Continuing almost guarantees that your destiny will be out of your hands – and Murphy's Law dictates that the boat inside you will make a lousy rounding and perhaps doom your whole race. Sacrifice a length or two now to eliminate that risk. Try to position yourself next to a lousy mark-rounder and sneak into the gap they gift to you.

Strangely, if you are at the back, this actually gives you a few aces to play. You can see the fleet, the gaps and the bunches to avoid. You get the gusts first and can use your wind shadow as a weapon. You have freedom to choose your own course rather than the others dictating to you. Just remember the rules forbid you blasting from behind into non-existent gaps.

To reiterate, positioning for the mark-rounding chaos is the priority. In turn, this depends on whether the inside berth comes with being to leeward or windward of the rest of the fleet. Either way it is almost inevitable that, in the fight for clear wind, the bulk of the fleet will have luffed each other well above the rhumb line and will be coming in sailing deep and slow. If you can come in high and fast, there is often a good chance that even with limited rights you can be clean away and gone while they are still hailing to deny you the room you did not need.

If, however, you are still stuck in the melee, it is drastic wriggle time. There is no benefit in sailing blithely to your doom. Instead, drop the kite early, centre the main, flap the jib and do everything you can to find yourself some space. It is inevitable that in the chaos, someone will make a lousy rounding, which is your opportunity to swoop. Notionally, yes, slowing actually loses you distance. But post-rounding you will have bought yourself freedom to tack or perhaps a controlling lane to sail in. The alternative was being trapped in dirty wind with little prospect of escape any time soon.

Finally, a word about asymmetrics. Plan properly and your need to sail the angles gives you an edge, particularly in a mixed fleet. Coming in fast on starboard for a port-hand rounding (or even vice-versa) theoretically gives you all the rights you need. In practice, that may not be the case – the (perhaps virtually stationary) fleet will probably not expect you and may simply not be able to get out of the way and provide your 'room'. So you need to anticipate this and start hailing early and clearly or you may find yourself shut out and disappointed.

In the following diagram, I've set out a typical downwind start scenario at the crucial time just before the three-lengths circle. What happen next depends on whether the mark is rounded to port or starboard.

On a port rounding, A and B are in in interesting little battle, with B heading higher to clear their wind from D and trying to get an overlap on A, who may need to respond by heading higher until they cut the three-length circle. X is beginning to heat up and could well overlap B in time, meaning that is B also overlaps A, X could round first. Y has it all to play for too. Starting late has left them at the back but they've avoided the luffing games, working low. With a much better angle, they should get F and back (who are all slowing each other) relatively easily. D and E are struggling for clear wind so are viable targets too and C's deep angle of approach means Y could actually round fourth. E needs to keep their sail in the gap between G and H but is horribly vulnerable to H blanketing them and sneaking low for an overlap. With the advantage of clear wind, H could round just after Y in fifth. The best hope for C, D and I is to keep going high, heading for the windward edge of the circle, tilting their transom extension lines away from the boats to leeward, protecting themselves from being overlapped. Once they hit the circle, they are safe.

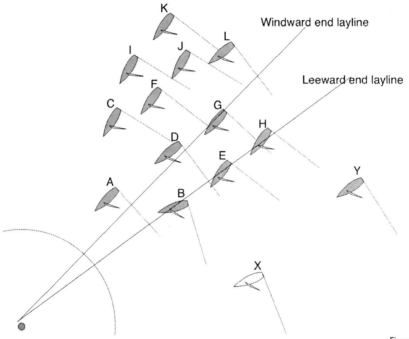

Figure 43

With D heading high and a bit of room to try and clear their air, G should head low, cement their place before the bunch to windward and be poised to swoop if D, E, H or even Y make a bad rounding. F is not in a good place; they will need to give room to perhaps six boats that will arrive at the same time and is vulnerable to J and L, with clear wind, gaining overlaps too. Why K and L would put themselves high and on the outside in this scenario, I have no idea, but it happens all the time. That's club racing for you. Quite possibly, they think the rounding is to starboard...

If it were, things look very different A is safe. B ought to be. X will hear lots of blathering about not having room, to which the answer should be 'catch me if you can'. If C is asleep, D may be able to luff and break their overlap, otherwise D's priority should be to shut out the rest and give themselves space for a decent rounding. As for the rest, with some many above the layline, the only certainty as that it will be chaos. So here is an exercise for you: what would you do if you were any each of the rest?

Over time, my approach to upwind starts has become very different from the conventional wisdom.

More than anything else, the priority is **clear air**, not so much at the moment the gun goes but over the following couple of minutes. This means crossing the line, in a nice gap, moving at least as quickly as the boats around you. The race is not decided half a second after the start gun, so being in pole position but stationary does little good.

With that clear air should come the freedom to chose which tack to sail on, because I want to be on the lifted tack asap.

These are the two key priorities.

Sure, I will check the line for bias and not fall into the trap of thinking it is the end closest to the mark that is favoured rather than the end closest to the wind. I like to get the feel by sailing close-hauled on starboard from the right-hand end and port from the left, then try and decide which tack will cross the other. I'll sail down the line with the mainsheet trimmed nicely and jammed then tack to see whether it is then under or over-sheeted (under-sheeted is favoured tack). Rarely will I use the compass – there is too much going on for mental arithmetic. I don't like shooting head-to either. It's – too easy to not actually be head-to after all – and who wants to get stuck in irons?

While knowing which end is favoured does influence my thinking, it doesn't dictate it. More than anything, I want to be on that   lifted tack as soon as possible. And if the wind shifts, which it may well at some point, the favoured end may well change with it.

Where starboard tack is lifted, decision-making is easier; be near the favoured end, but unless I am confident there will not be a jam-up I will not risk winning pole-position. I have been taken out too many times. Instead I will be more conservative and make sure I have a nice lane to sail in, preferably between people/boats I can roll but who are unlikely to roll me.

If port is the lifted tack, it gets trickier. I really do not want to be trapped on the headed starboard tack, unable to get onto lifted port, so the pin is probably out, unless a cheeky flier is achievable (which it can be on an under-populated fixed club-line). If it is a big header (regardless of line bias) I will happily start on port, ducking anyone in the way. Anything to be on the lifted tack (figure 45).

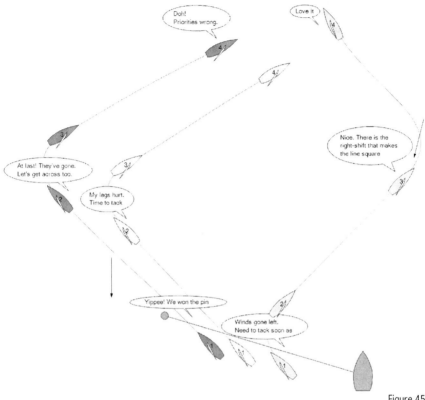

Figure 45

In some races, line bias is irrelevant of course. In a contrary tide, the only thing that matters can be getting out of the channel to the favoured side of the beat. If the tide is pushing you over, the main priority is to avoid being OCS (getting back against the tide will be horrible) and after that it is often a matter of locking onto the stream and not worrying so much about anything else. The relevance of tide depends on its strength compared to the wind speed. Two knots of each and tide is the priority, but in a slackish tide on a windy day other factors will likely take precedence

When I am coaching, we spend what may seem to be a disproportionate amount of time practising starts, keeping everyone within a small, defined box, but it pays massive dividends. The greatest impediment to decent starts is often a reluctance to get in there and mix it. This almost guarantees a second-row start, dirty wind and a doomed race. The anticipation, however, is often worse than the event. So if you are a shy starter, bite the bullet. Chances are that most of the rest are struggling with their boat handling too. Vow to get in there and mix it but avoid lining up next to a hotshot.

A quick reminder of the salient rules:

- Windward does have to keep clear but if you come in from behind and underneath, you have to give them time and opportunity to keep clear. If the boat to weather is constrained by several others, so cannot move up, you cannot force yourself into a leeward gap that is not there.

- You cannot call for water on a committee boat or the pin. In Fowey Regatta Week, prevailing winds mean the committee boat is usually at the port end with the line set from the middle of that large vessel. If you cannot get around the mooring line at the front, tough; a boat to windward is under no obligation to you at all. Do not start in that triangle of doom; it can only end in tears. (figure 46)

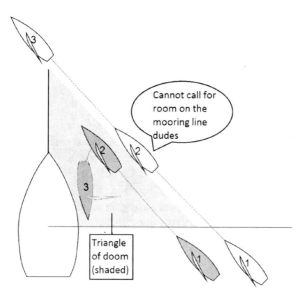

Figure 46

- Boats going backwards have no rights. Don't go backwards!

- More conventionally, boats on the starboard tack lay-line to the right-hand end do not have to let in boats reaching in from on high. Please do not be the comedian that tries that one on. (figure 47)

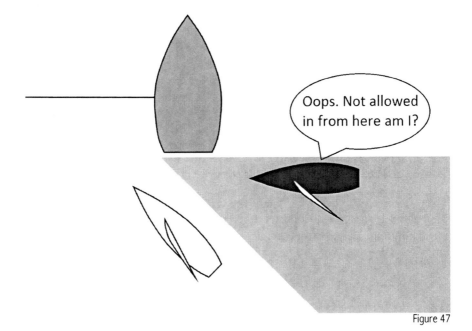

Figure 47

After the start

How often have we all seen one of the club also-rans have a dream first leg, or even lap, right at the front of the fleet? Up there, it all seems much easier and they sometimes hang in for quite a while. Then one boat gets past, then another and another until all of a sudden they are on the steep slippery slope back to Averageville. Why, why, why?

It may have been a fluke that they were at the front at all and this time, banging a corner they lucked-out big time. The law of averages balances out eventually, but that only explains a proportion of the times this happens. If someone can sail the first leg or three as well as any hotshot, why not the remainder?

There are two reasons. One is the syndrome first identified by Timothy Galwey in The Inner Game of Tennis athat we covered earlier.

The other is a lack of that key factor the top guys all have: relentlessness. They never let up, they are always doing the right thing and every time we normal human beings make a small error, they draw away a foot or a boat-length or 10 – until we cannot read their sail numbers anymore.

CLUB SAILORS UP THE BEAT

There is so much to do. Keep it flat, hike, hike, hike. Keep it moving at top VMG. Work out what the wind is doing and which way to go. Keep to a lane with clear wind. Sail the fleet or go your own way? Balance strategy and tactical requirements. Negotiate the chop/waves/tide. Adjust rig controls to suit gusts and lulls. Keep an eye open for converging boats. Plan approach to windward mark. Ignore the aches in legs/arms/ wherever. Keep the concentration up. Keep the spirits up if things are not going so well. Keep the euphoria locked up if it is; the race is not over until you hear that finish signal.

Of course, it is simply not possible to micro-manage every one of these, every second. You need to prioritise – and that is often the hardest part: choosing what is most important, going with it and keeping everything else bubbling along.

Windshifts: Cutting the circles

Many people I have coached have found this a really good way to think about windshifts.

Imagine lots of concentric circles drawn on the water, centred on a windward mark. Like this:

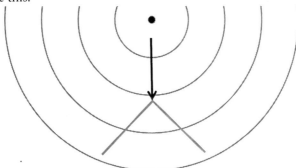

If the beat is completely square to the wind, irrespective of the tack you are on, the boat will be cutting those circles as it sails along at the same rate (until you get to the lay-line of course).

If the wind now shifts say 30 degrees one way (huge I know, but it makes understanding easier) on one tack you will be sailing almost straight at the mark cutting those circles like crazy (shown as the solid lines in the diagram below). Whereas on the other tack, you will be sailing almost perpendicular to the rhumb-line, getting no closer to the mark and cutting virtually no circles (shown as the dotted lines).

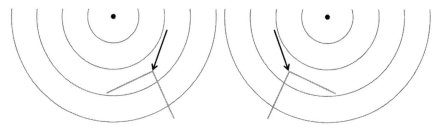

Comparing two paths, one always on the lifted tack, cutting circles, the other on the header is enlightening, with the headed path taking nearly six times as far.

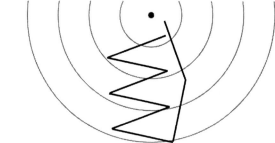

Hence we get to the essence: if in doubt, sail the tack that takes you closest to the mark.

The same principle applies even in a more realistic ten-degree windshift – and you should still be able to visualise cutting those circles at different rates.

Having established this, all things being equal (ignoring tides, wind-bends et al) a fantastic rule of thumb is to do everything you can to make sure you are always on the tack that cuts the concentric circles fastest.

Following this principle has a couple of other benefits. It can stop you nailing yourself right out to the corners. And on a beat that is not square from the outset, it will push you to do the long leg first, which is almost always the right thing. In figure 51, on the left Grey takes the short tack first, but it heads them near the mark, allowing white to cross them and overtake. On the right, the set up is the same only the wind lifts near the mark, allowing

White to make it in one. Grey wasted two boat lengths hitching to the left early and again White gets past.

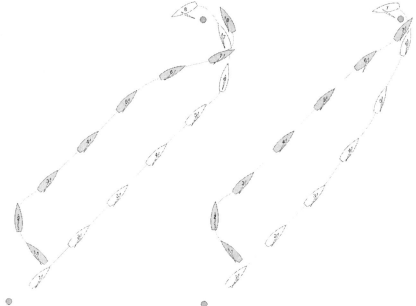

Figure 51

Of course, if you have an asymmetric, the same principles apply downwind where you will need to gybe at some point. Just be sure you compare headings based on true wind direction rather than on the apparent wind effect. And remember, pressure is usually more important than a shift.

More on windshifts

We can generally categorise windshifts into four types:

1. An oscillating breeze that switches back and forth, typically 10 to 15 degrees. For example the wind bearing might be 220 degrees or 230 degrees, but not much else. I tend to think of this as a tick-tock wind as it flicks back and forth every few minutes.
2. A breeze that wobbles erratically within a range about a mean (average).
3. A persistent over-riding swing in one direction, perhaps overlaid with smaller periodic shifts as above.
4. A bend generated by a geographical feature. This will feel like type (3) above as you sail into it but like (1) or (2) if you stayed in the same place.

The best approach depends on which type you face:

1. Be alert and always on the right tick or tock, in clear wind.
2. Look up and see whether the clouds can be correlated with the wobbles. Work out the mean heading. This is the key. Try to stay on the better-than-mean tack, but if in doubt (or it is at mean) get back to the rhumb-line of the beat.
3. If the wind is continually swinging left, sail left first (or vice-versa). It is not uncommon for the wind to swing around with the sun but that all happens quite slowly of course. The more likely cause is an impending weather front.
4. Sail into the bend so you get progressively headed. If you do not go far enough, you will not get the long beneficial lift on the way back out. Sadly not all OODs position the course to enable you to use a bend to the utmost. Spoilsports.

    Do not overstand the windward mark as you get lifted out – you will need to tack below what appears to be the lay-line to allow for the geographical lift to come.

Managing the rest of the fleet in windshifts is about leverage (a.k.a. separation). If you are very close to your competitors, getting a small shift right or wrong will not make a huge difference. Conversely, if you hit the left corner on a one-mile beat, when everyone else goes right, an adverse shift will leave you perhaps hundreds of yards down. Race over. Assess the risk as you would for gambling on horses – is it a £5 bet on a 3:2 chance (unlikely to wipe you out), or betting the farm on a 250-to-1 outsider (otherwise known as lunacy)?

Do not get me wrong – leverage can be your ally. It is perfectly possible in the right circumstances to create a gain from nothing other than the knowledge that a header (or bend) will appear. In figure 53, black gets the bow down and sails fast and low, confident a header is on the way. Two boat-lengths of new leverage converts to a gain as soon as that header arrives. Even if white tacks on the header too, black now has the upper hand.

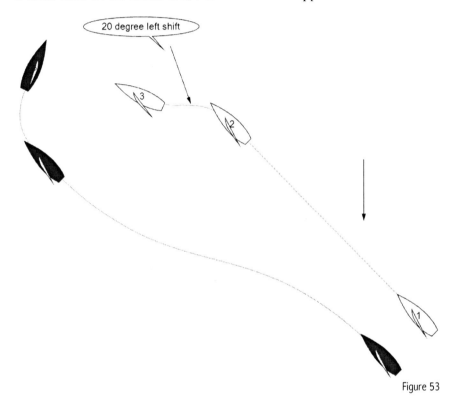

Figure 53

TEN WAYS TO SPOT A HEADING SHIFT

1. The hotshots ahead will all tack in turn as the shift reaches them.

2. The same tack boats that were ahead and to leeward will now appear to be dead-ahead or even to windward of you. The same tack boats behind will now look further to leeward.

3. More opposite tack boats come into view around your bow.

4. Opposite tack boats that it seemed you would cross may now look like they can cross you.

5. Compass bearings will change – on starboard they will decrease, and on port they will increase.

6. Landmarks ahead will move to windward (to the right on starboard and vice versa).

7. The dark patch on the water from an approaching gust is coming more from ahead than 45 degrees

8. Waves will be coming at the bow at a different angle.

9. The windward tell-tales may stop streaming as the shift hits.

10. The boat may heel to windward as the power comes out of the no-longer 100% trimmed sails.

If the opposite happens then you have a lift not a header.

CLUB SAILORS ON THE REACH

Yeah. This is the life. Planing along at full speed, spray everywhere. Exhilarating or what? But in race terms, does anything much change? Maybe the fleet spreads out a bit. Perhaps a few drop it in at a gybe mark. In reality, though, aren't reaches just space fillers – a join-the-dots requirement between beats?

Not necessarily. The fastest course is seldom a completely straight line, whether it is light, windy, tight or broad, flat or wavy. Most club sailors will simply point the boat at the next mark, maybe trim the sails now and then, but otherwise switch off.

So there is still plenty of room for you to make some gains. Intuitively, we know that heading up tends to put some speed on, while going low tends to be slower. This, of course, is the thing that encourages the boat behind to try to overtake us by going high of the layline.

Equally, it feels all a lot less sluggish sailing low in a gust compared to a lull.

Applying these two principles in turn will virtually always get you to the next mark more quickly than sailing a straight line. The increase in speed will more than compensate for that bit of extra distance.

Head up a bit in the lulls to keep the speed on. Work lower in the puffs, staying in the pressure longer and building the opportunity to come higher when it has gone, so increasing the overall VMG. If you find yourself low, still with good pressure as the mark looms, all well and good - you will be piling on the gains, sailing far faster than anyone else.

If you can get the boat planing, really go for it. Pump (within the rules!). Move aft as you accelerate and the boat does come onto the plane and then use the increased apparent wind to get lower, without losing the plane obviously. At the end of the gust, head up to keep on that bow-wave a bit longer. When it is finished, move forward again to readjust the trim and stop the transom dragging.

Approaching the mark, concentrate like crazy to make sails, trim, balance and any waves work for you to earn that vital couple of inches of overlap that effectively gives you an overtake. But please do not pump and rock illegally to achieve that end – this is not a rowing race, after all.

Asymmetric sailors; do not forget the centreboard! . Since it gets left down when the kite is up to prevent lee-helm, it tends to be ignored on a white-sail-only reach. But it does not need to be fully down creating drag for no reason; get some of it out of the way.

CLUB SAILORS ON THE RUN

At last. Time to relax? Er, no. Particularly as that is what the rest of your competitors are likely to be doing. So where can we nick a few lengths then? or several places?

Firstly, use some forethought that you can apply while still on the beat. Windshift-wise, if starboard is the lifted tack coming into the windward mark, you will want to be on port as soon as possible for the run (but avoiding sailing into the wind shadow of the starboard lay-line queue still on the beat). If port tack was the final lifted tack, you will want to start the run on starboard. Of course, wind bends, wind shadows, tides and currents may over-rule the shift, but either way you should know on the approach whether you plan to gybe. Most will not think this far ahead, so you can get the jump on them.

Secondly, make a good rounding. Control lines eased in advance, windward heel and fast ease of the mainsheet would be ideal. Too many people sail two or three lengths on a beam-reach before the boat is actually pointed toward the next mark. That is two or three lengths thrown away – do not do this unless aggressively protecting yourself from a rival behind.

Thirdly, eyes back. Because you are now sailing away from, rather than into the wind, shifts come along only about a third as often. But pressure (windspeed) is really important down the run and it tends to come in streaks. So keep looking behind and get yourself in the dark water. Looking back will also enable you to see other boats and ensure you position yourself away from others' wind shadows.

Fourth: sailing down the run in flat water is a time when using the rudder really is bad news. Use heel and sail-trim instead for steering.

Next: waves. How we love 'em! Seek out YouTube video examples of the top guys sailing waves and see how radical the course direction changes are. Also note how hard they are working the rig – but if you're watching Ben in a Finn, remember that over a certain wind speed in Finn races they can be freed to pump as much as they like. You are not! Just keep pointing the boat downhill as much as possible, treating the uphill bits as obstacles to avoid. Practise, practise, practise. Improve your proficiency and you can make miles.

Next: as all crews know, if you only take your eyes off the spinnaker for a millisecond over a run, that is when it will collapse. So get the crew to concentrate on it exclusively while simultaneously providing a running commentary to the helm; how the sheet load feels (light/powered up) whether you can bear-off or need to come up to keep things at the optimum angle. This does not come easily to some but get them to persevere – and the helm needs to listen and respond accordingly. As the helm is looking backwards for the gusts, the chat needs to go the other way too, letting the crew know a gust is approaching, or the breeze is about to go soft.

Next: know your angles. Heading downhill with the wind precisely astern is seldom the best way. Every boat has a sweet angle where the air flows around the rig rather than going for an HMS Victory, square-rigger-style push-along effect. Inevitably, the angle varies across boats and even across the wind-spectrum. Sometimes in the RS200, the deep-soakers and the high-speed-reachers make the same VMG – very confusing!

Finally: gybes! Keeping the rig pointing upwards is always a good start point, but that's hardly an ideal capability peak. In all but the most extreme weather, if you avoid gybing for fear of it going wrong, you are likely to be sailing on the wrong shift at least part of the time (perhaps all of it). So go out there when it does not matter and analyse and practise your technique until this becomes a non-issue.

Perhaps the run is not time for feet-up and a breather after all!

MORE ON DOWNWIND SAILING

It has been said before, but it needs saying again, with emphasis: ***turning downwind is not an excuse for rest and relaxation!!***

There are great gains (and losses) to be made downwind. Sometimes, it is true, pottering along a reach can be a bit processional, with everyone going at roughly the same speed. But there are plenty of ways to break from the crowd.

Strategy

Boats may indeed all travel at much the same speed, but *only* if going in the same direction, with the same amount of pressure (wind). Conversely, we have all sat in frustration when another boat gets a gust and planes off while we are going nowhere. This illustrates how pressure is king. Rather like a pantomime villain, *'It's behind you'* – but behind us is not where we tend to look. We should – because if you can just change your observation habits your downwind performance can leap. When Roger Gilbert comes for a Laser sail with us at Frensham, it is noticeable that he spends significantly more time on a run looking over the transom than anywhere else. So hunt the pressure and get yourself in front of the dark streaks. Some may remember Dennis Connor was the first US skipper to lose the America's Cup; missing a wind streak on a run was how he did it.

There is also a difference here between a fast boat and a slower one. In a slower boat, the gusts will be catching you up. But in a high performance machine, it can be the other way around - you can actually catch the gusts ahead.

Particularly in a dinghy, a straight line downwind is seldom the fastest route between two points. Instead, try making more use of the gusts and lulls. In the lulls the boat goes slower, so head up a bit and keep the boat moving. When the gust comes, bear back down below the rhumb line. That way you will keep the speed on and stay in the gust for longer. Getting low is money in the bank, allowing you to head up and really pile the speed on towards the end of the leg when you get to the pinch point of the mark.

If you are a puddle sailor like me, by definition windward marks are of necessity near the windbreak that is the shore. If you are in this situation, a core objective is to get out into the undisturbed, stronger air as soon as possible.

Club sailors rarely race way out in the open sea – and the closer to the shore we are, the more the chance of wind bends, hotspots and dead-zones. Watch your club hotshots. If they always go the same way in specific conditions, making use of one or more of these will be the reason why. If in doubt, ask them after the race. Most are happy to share their knowledge and help you understand what was happening. Do not be fooled because occasionally it does not pay for them. Mostly, it will; that is why they do it and why you should too.

If you sail somewhere tidal or where there are nice waves to play with, both of these need to be factored into your strategy. So get to where they help you, avoid them where they hinder. The stronger their effect, the more radical you can be.

Tactics

Have you ever noticed how a fleet will quite often sail a great circle route downwind? Each boat behind creeps higher, so the one in front defends by coming up too until, approaching the mark, they are all now on a snail-rate run, paying for the early reaching. Being one of the lemmings is not compulsory, but it does take courage to break free – to break away to leeward and sail your own fastest course. If being leeward gives you the inside line at the next mark, you have an extra advantage – not only will you be approaching on a faster angle, away from the dirty wind of the bunch, but you will be calling water too – their low angle definitely giving you your overlap. If you can foresee chaos, start making your presence known early – they tend to be wrapped up in their own local battles and there is nothing worse than being squeezed out through weight of numbers no matter how 'in the right' you are.

If you will be on the outside at the next mark, you may need to be a bit more circumspect or could find yourself rounding outside everyone else. Break low if you can get clear wind, but if you do anticipate being trapped on the outside, start coming up and mixing it well before the 3 lengths circle.

I sometimes find it amazing, particularly with relative beginners and at the back off the fleet, that boats are drawn together as if by gravity. In a bunch is not a good place to be, particularly on a run – because the wind treats all those sails as a barrier and tries to find a way around it. If you suffer from this syndrome, resolve to take steps to move away from the others in future. You do not need them slowing you down.

In all this, the common factor is clear wind. If you are in mid-fleet and someone is bugging you, politely point out you will both get there faster if you sail the fleet not each other or ask if they'd like you, in return, to sit on them all the way up the beat. Otherwise, make an aggressive manoeuvre to clear your wind and let them know you will not accept any nonsense. Bear in mind that it is a bit naïve to expect this gambit to work on the penultimate leg when you are leading! Hypocrisy is not a good thing either – so do unto others…

ROUNDING MARKS

"Ye canna change the laws of physics, Captain". The same principle applies to mark roundings as to Scotty's famous 'Star Trek' remark.

Leeward mark

Opportunities to make a nice gain, opportunities to throw all that hard work away...

In the diagram below, too close alongside the mark, Black is set up all wrong, so will have to use too much rudder in the turn, slowing the boat dramatically. Momentum will also throw the boat to leeward and in the inevitable panic the sails will simply get pulled in as quickly as possible, so will be either over or under-sheeted all through the turn. You can be fairly sure that resetting the rig controls for the beat has been forgotten too. Hopefully, the plate is actually down, but it ain't necessarily so. Once hardened up onto the breeze, a look over the shoulder will show the skipper they are at least one or perhaps three boat lengths to leeward of the mark. Oh dear. You don't want to do it like that.

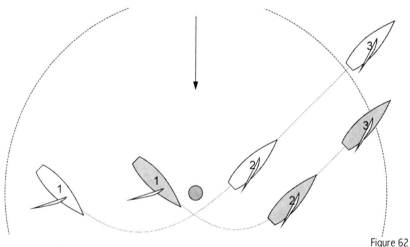

Figure 62

By contrast, the white sets up nicely wide of the mark, a point they have perhaps been aiming at for some time, having recognised they were never going to get an overlap. With lots of room, they can go for a smooth turn, using much less (braking-effect) rudder. The sails come in smoothly, being set perfectly to the wind throughout the turn. With far less stress in the boat, the control lines will likely to be adjusted in a timely fashion too. The only danger is actually catching chaotic Black before the mark, so getting trapped on the outside of them and forced miles wide – so they watch like hawks for further muppetry and ease the main to slow up a bit if necessary and cement the inside track. Immediately after rounding, White will be to weather of their rivals. A few lengths later, having accelerated through the turn rather than slowed, they are likely to be ahead too.

So guess which boat is Toast and which is Butter, smooth, slippery and soon all over them? Tasty.

Your every leeward rounding should be set up like Butter here, even (particularly) if there is no other boat within shouting distance. For the ultimate rounding, also remember:

- Leeward heel will help the turn.
- The process of sheeting on the main will bring the boat up into the wind.
- Conversely, over-zealous sheeting-on of the jib will have the opposite effect, which is not helpful – so if anything the jib can afford to be a split second tardy. What we do not want is the jib to be simply slammed into its close-hauled position in one clumsy, rapid yank in advance of the turn.
- Which order is best, then, for multiple jobs? I'd propose:
    - Board down – rounding-up is embarrassing with the plate hidden in its case.
    - Outhaul.
    - Rig tension.
    - Stow the kite such that, even if not quite 100% away, there is absolutely no chance of it going trawling for fish or of lines ending up under the boat.
    - Most of the kicker – but not too soon before or the boat will noticeably slow – you have to actually get to the mark after all.
    - A bit of cunningham if it will be required (too much, too soon and you really will stop dead, mind).

    - Once close-hauled, fine tune kicker and cunno.

- But – if it is really really tonking out there, I'd personally accept a bit of lost speed a boat length or two before the mark to hit the beat all set-up, controlled and flat.

- Which way you want to go – something you ought to have at least considered whilst in the last few downwind lengths. If 'the other way' (left on a port-hand rounding, right for a starboard rounding) is favoured, freedom to tack is paramount. Just remember the boats still coming downwind. Their dirty wind is bad enough. Worse, crashing into someone is easily done in all the excitement too, so pick your path with care.

Part of the reason sailing is the ultimate sport is that the real world is way more complicated than diagrams in books. Marks sometimes have multitudes of boats arriving at the same time so are a great example of this. Many of your competitors will have, most selfishly, also read books, thought deeply about things and learned from hard experience. What rotten, spoilsport so-and-so's. Worse, some will have an incomplete knowledge of the rules, will still be working off the 1968 version or may appear to have learned a set transported from a parallel universe. Then there will be the hotshots who you can rely on to do what is the right thing for them – making your job even harder in the process. Mixed in will be someone who is completely unpredictable, could do things like a champ but also could drop a clanger and force you somewhere you really do not want to go.

What to do then? When a melee is inevitable, the key is to have your head out of the boat, so get all the controls and distractions sorted in advance. Avoid marginal 'room' calls, as there is never enough time to argue and the cost of any disagreement is untenable. Have a look around and where it is absolutely clear, politely say 'no room' or 'after you' as applicable. Then have a polite chat with those where it is more marginal. Where you have taken the initiative, they may well not argue with you! Now you know where you stand (as best you can anyway) visualise how many will be rounding before you, how much time and space you will need to give, then wriggle, slow or accelerate so you can make a clean rounding when it is your turn. Keep an eye open for late-late chancers (there is always one!) and make it clear there are no vacancies, they needed to book earlier. Given this is a game of dodgems, expect the unexpected. Make sure you (do not drop)/keep hold of (*positive thoughts only please*) your tiller extension and sheet – the objective is to sail serenely through the chaos, not create more.

When carnage does ensue, as it will sometimes:

- Do not use hands, arms or legs as fenders – they are poorly designed for this function and trips to hospital interfere with après-sail time.

- If you can avoid boat and people damage *without* acting as a fender, say by handing-off shrouds, fair play. The heavier the boat and the faster it is going, the less chance such interventions will go well. If in doubt, keep your hands in. Instead, think how the insurance claim will transfer value from the financial sector to the marine sector, which has to be a good thing.

- But do not do what we once suffered at a Cannes 470 event – someone who failed to give us room grabbed our shrouds and pulled themselves forward, us back. I had to refrain my helm from repelling boarders with the spinnaker pole.

- If you infringed through no fault of your own, make that fact clear to whomever you fouled and make sure the guilty party gets spinning. Rather than being caught in the middle, it's better to yell 'protest' there and then, protecting yourself from getting pinged in the protest room later.

- If it is your fault, admit it, find some space and get dizzy. If you can, make sure they see you doing so. If local rules require, declare your 720 on signing-off sheets.

- No matter whose fault any nonsense was, put it out of your mind and focus on the rest of the race straightaway. Take a deep breath or three, count to 10, sing a calming song in your head and focus on being rational and analytical. The only thing that matters is to get up the next leg in the least time possible, starting from where you actually are, not where you think you should have been.

- If others are still shouting, fantastic, they are focused on the wrong thing. This gives you an edge, an opportunity. Ignore their histrionics and make the most of the gift they are giving you. Lovely.

Windward mark

Compared with leeward marks, the windward mark should be relatively easy. Yeah, right.

I sometimes think the main problems at windward marks come from unrealistic optimism combined with apparent ignorance of Murphy's Law. You know, 'I was a bit below the lay-line, but I was sure I could shoot it, until it headed me at the last minute'. Or 'The tide was much stronger at the mark'. More likely the flow assessment was lousy. Or even 'A big gust arrived just as I was rounding and the boom hit it'.

Although the remedy to these is obvious, covered by the common sense advice to sail the conditions as they are, rather than as you think they should be, there will still be scope for incident, fun and games. A good source of opportunity flows from the rules.

Time flies; it was in 1997 that the rule rewrite (a.k.a. simplification) significantly reduced the rights of a boat tacking within two (now three) lengths of a windward mark. As I write in 2011, 14 years later, it seems to me that at least half of most fleets remain ignorant of this one. Further, whilst conceptually it is straightforward, in practice it can become quite complex, particularly on starboard roundings.

The easiest way to stay on the right side of the rule is simply never to tack within three lengths of a windward mark if there is going to be another boat approaching who came from outside that circle. In the real world, we overstand, get pushed to the lay-line by others, or strategic or tactical considerations (tides, wind shadows and bends, big shifts) force our hand. So what's to be done? Usually you have to concede to the approaching boat(s). In a big fleet, coming in on a port lay-line could see you duck nearly everyone. Expensive.

The rules say you can tack (as in complete your tack) on the lay-line in front of an approaching boat and be OK as long as, in subsequently avoiding you, they do not have to sail above close-hauled. In other words, you are relying on them having over-stood it and still being high enough to sail above you without windward tell-tales lifting on sheeted-in sails. This could be tricky to prove, particularly as you will be looking in the opposite direction.

A starboard rounding is a real rules tease, but ultimately logical. If two boats are converging on their respective lay-lines to a starboard rounded mark, the starboard boat has right of way – the mark is ignored. However, the starboard boat will have to tack at some point to round. Once tacking, they have to keep clear, again as if the mark was not there. Having completed the tack, the rule about tacking within the three-lengths circle kicks-in, just as for a port-hand rounding described above.

This brings interesting tactical options for each. For the starboard-tacker, the mean trick that is forcing the port-tacker to tack will probably work but personally I don't like it – what goes around comes around, after all. It tends to all look something like the figure 67 below.

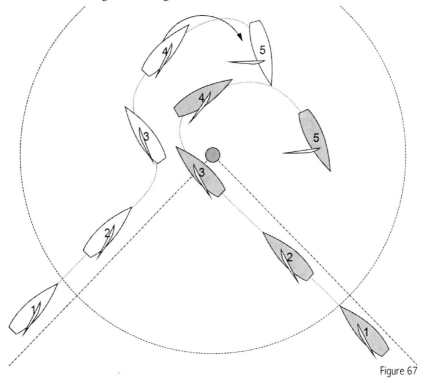

Figure 67

The remaining options are to cross then tack clear to windward or tack in front if you can and they are clearly over-standing. Remember that the objective is to be in the controlling position after the mark rounding – no point winning a skirmish to lose the battle.

If you are the port boat and you are sure they will force you to tack (some people are so predictable) the best option perhaps is to get down to your lay-line and slow down so they **have** to cross you, then you are through underneath them and away (fugure 68).

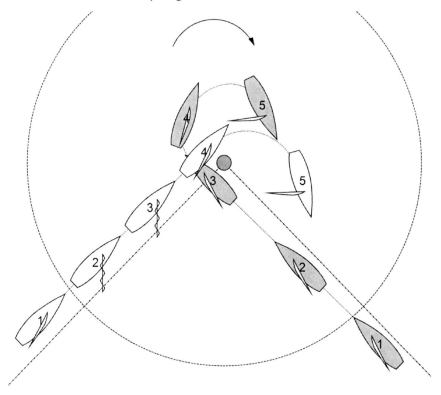

Figure 68

Alternatively, head high and invite them to tack inside you – at which point you roll over them and take control that way (Figure 69).

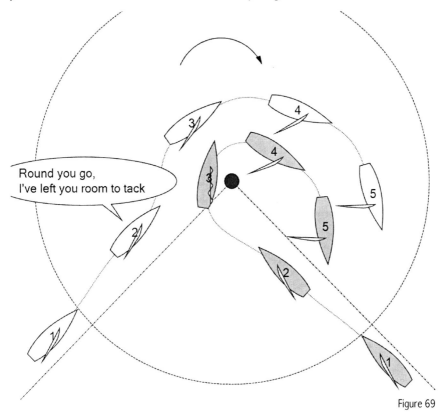

Round you go,
I've left you room to tack

Figure 69

This all makes it sounds like the port-tacker has the edge – which is after all the intention of the rule – to discourage tacking within the circle.

There is often confusion too on starboard roundings when two same-tack boats both approach on starboard at or above the lay-line. The rules are quite simple in this instance: the windward boat is entitled to room if overlapped at three lengths, just like at any other mark.

Now we have got matters outside the boat covered, what about inside. The bear-away is a big deal in some boats, but in any case it is worthwhile at least getting the kicker off before rounding (or you might find the boat will not actually bear away at all). If you can do the other controls without prejudicing actually rounding the thing, then go for it. When you get there, get that mainsheet out to help the turn and use some windward heel for the same reason. Save raising the board until you are around though.

In the light stuff, do not forget the effect of your momentum on the apparent wind. Countless times, I have seen people bear off and push the boom out hard to where it should be for the new run. In response, the main promptly backwinds and the boat stops, regardless of the fact that the leg is a run – or more accurately will become one once the boat slows to running speed and the apparent wind rebalances itself. Yes, ease the sheets to help the turn, but let the boom go no faster than its own pace.

The next thing that happens is that the crew jumps up and frantically starts hoisting kites. This is fine in a decent wind. But if it's all light and flighty, being smooth and gentle is the order of the day; no dancing elephants allowed. On a puddle like my home club, a windward mark is almost by definition in the wind shadow of the ~~weeds~~ trees. The priority is to get the blazes out of there and into the pressure. Shaking the wind out of the sails to hoist a spinny that is not yet going to fill is not the best way. Get out of there first; the mark rounding is not over until the new equilibrium is established and you are properly on your way to the next mark.

Gybe mark

Gybe marks in club races often throw up different challenges from that of the Olympic triangle. We round them to starboard. We go from fetch to fetch and all sorts of other combinations. However, some constants remain. Priority One is to keep your own mast pointing towards the sky. Priority Two is to avoid being taken out by another boat that failed to adhere to Priority One. Priority Three: decide if gybing is actually the best thing. In many instances, keeping going can be the fast thing to do, perhaps for tidal considerations, to get into more pressure or simply to keep clear wind from the rest of the fleet. Think for yourself rather than follow mindlessly.

In the approach, many of the same principles apply as to the leeward mark. Planning the exit is predominately about positioning for advantage on the next leg. If the next leg is a fetch, you need to be high for clear wind. If being to windward puts you on the inside at the following mark, you need a strong argument to be low on the fleet.

Whether you want to be low or high on the next leg dictates the rounding style. If you need to be high, again it is a case of 'in wide, out tight'. If you want to be low but are in a bunch, take great care. The more boats that arrive at the mark together, the greater the likelihood of a post-rounding luffing match. If one boat rolls you in the process, there is a big risk they all will, leaving you floundering in useless, dirty air having lost several places. The safe options are therefore to keep going rather than gybe at all, or join in with the shenanigans until things stabilise and you can break low with reasonably clear wind. Neither is ideal; the boats clear ahead of this nonsense will be making the most of sailing an optimal course and consolidating their lead. Conversely, if you can see it happening ahead of you, rub your hands together in glee. Sail optimally while they all slow each other down and you could get yourself right back into the mix by the next mark.

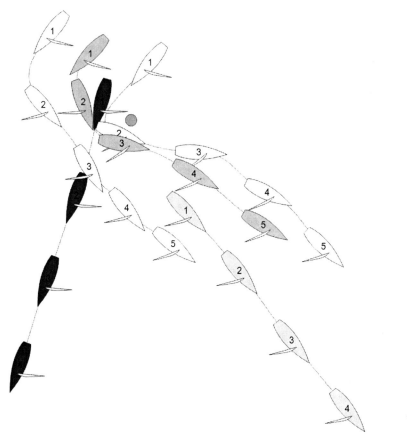

Figure 72

Figure 72 above shows a fraction of the chaos that can occur. White has got pushed wide and been rolled by the boats requiring room and is now moving at half their speed. More boats, not shown in the diagram, will probably overtake too. The leader is well away, no doubt chuckling to themselves. Black foresaw the luffing matches to come so decided not to gybe. They could well look good later.

THE DREADED WINDY GYBE

If there is one manoeuvre that club sailors dread, it has to be the windy-day gybe, often featuring the freestyle capsize as a punctuation mark. No longer.

When it comes to windy gybes, there are broadly three sailor groups: those who rarely have a problem, those who can gybe successfully until the pressure of a race situation interjects and those who invariably capsize.

Full marks to the first group. The second group should re-read the section about the Inner Game and remember to always think positive: think "Stay upright" rather than "Don't fall in". Then analyse technique and identify where the flaw is hiding. With me it is being thrown off balance at a crucial moment. Getting someone knowledgeable in the safety boat to watch you can be useful too.

For the third group, we need to return to basics. If the boat is not balanced and broadly under control as you approach the gybe, the chances of a happy outcome are not good. Do everything you can, including waiting a bit, to normalise things. Ensure the controls are as they should be and that the centreboard is in the right place. Sheet the main in first to reduce the required direction change required to ensure the boom will cross. Spinnaker boats can sometimes switch the jib sheet in advance of the gybe; falling in solely because of a neglected jib is frankly silly.

If the boat is still accelerating from a new gust, rig loads will be increasing; so it's better to wait until the boat is at top speed when the loads will have actually reduced. If there are waves, gybe on the way down when sometimes the surfing speed can reduce the power in the rig to virtually nothing.

The bigger the angle the boat needs to be turned through to persuade the boom to come across, the greater the risk when it does. Paradoxically, however, to make the boat turn we need to break it out of that precious stability, which means being bold and firm. Going into the gybe, the objective is to do enough to get the boom to decide *irrevocably* that it is going to cross. This may mean a determined action with the rudder and a jerk at the right moment on the mainsheet, gybing strop or kicker. Keep an eye on the top batten at the leech; it will be twitching when it is ready to come. Once that boom is moving, swift action is required: by the time it reaches the new side you need to be on the new windward side, ready to bang down with all of your weight if needs must. At the same time, as soon as the boom is on the move, rapidly adjust to steer back down towards a run, taking the sting out of the rig. Hence the course steered will be, roughly, an S shape, comprising a curve to induce the gybe, an opposite curve to remove the sting, then heating back up as you settle on to the new course. In an asymmetric the final return of the S should not be necessary but you need to exit the gybe at the right angle.

If the boom feels like it will come but something changes and it becomes clear it will not, do not force it. Get things rebalanced and try again.

Beware the chop created by other boats. Try and find yourself space and clear, undisturbed water.

Remember that the anticipation is often worse than the event. You can gybe in a Force 1 – this is just stronger and faster. So be strong and quick yourself.

When it does go wrong, how annoying is it to fall in, get back upright and still have to make the gybe? If you do drop it in, can you sail the thing around to avoid this scenario? Or allow it to blow over the other way, nip across the boat and right again quickly.

In extremis, there is nothing wrong with wearing (tacking) around. Expedience is perfectly acceptable. Take care though to sail sufficiently past a gybe-mark that you have room to bear away again and leave the mark on the required side. If it is sufficiently windy to wear around, the bear-away may not be the easiest manoeuvre either. Note the words 'in extremis'. We are only talking about club races. Bottling out every time will cost you distance, places and create a ballooning psychological block. That would be a shame. Of all the things we do in sailing a small boat, a well-executed windy gybe is the one most likely to give you that fist pumping, euphoric "YES" when it goes well.

Having absorbed this gybing advice, you may not want to bother with the next section.

CAPSIZING

Thorny issue this one, eh? With some boats, a capsize means pretty much race over. In others like a Laser it is usually no big deal.

We also have to consider the fact that, quite often, the closer to the edge you sail, the faster you go. So when should you push and when is it right to be expedient? To keep that big stick pointing upwards at all costs?

Clearly, it depends on the race and the objectives. If you have not seen the 'crash and burn' video of the Beijing 49er medal race it is well worth finding (try youtube.com). The issue there was perhaps deciding what expedient actually was. Generally though, leading the last leg of a medal race when you have a decent buffer is a time to be pragmatic, whereas if it is do or die to get from fourth to first overall there, we'd all go for it.

As a club racer, it is different though. Olympians practise for hours and hours, year after year. We club sailors rarely if ever practise. But is a race so important that we should always do the conservative thing? Many spinnakers would virtually never get hoisted in that case – so why have one?

I would argue that we only get to live this life once, so just go for it, unless it really is the last lap of a series clincher. Look on the bright side, when it all does go horribly wrong you get to practise two things – the sailing and the capsize recovery. Also, during racing there should be some safety cover, whereas going out unaccompanied (particularly on the sea) is a much higher risk tariff.

Hopefully you have decided to really have a go. But there are still things to be done to make sure you avoid that costly swim in the first place:

- Keep a weather eye open for the gusts – be ready and act as appropriate to keep upright. Anticipation is half the battle.

- Hike like crazy when the time comes. Bounce on the gunwale, even get one foot on the plate. Fight to keep that mast out of the water if there is any chance of saving it.

- Do not fight a lost cause though – better to gracefully step onto the plate and stay in some control, ready to right, than fall in the water and need to start swimming about – the recovery will be far slower and swimming is so disrespectful to a billion years of your ancestors' evolutionary struggle.

- Downwind
  - Ease the kicker sufficiently to stop the boom catching in the water (but not so little that uncontrollable twist rolls you in to windward).
  - Sit back to keep from nose-diving.
  - In a gust, if all else fails, ease the mainsheet, bear off, fold the kite's leading edge or even let the sheet go completely.
  - Bearing away with leeward-heel converts the rudder-blade into a wing, lifting the transom and digging the bows in: everything is then fighting everything else. Do not let things go so far that this syndrome kicks in.
- Upwind
  - Ease sheets. Pinch up to de-power (definitely do NOT bear off with the sails pinned in).
  - If all else fails, just let everything go, tiller, sheets, the lot. The boat will naturally swing head-to-wind. You may end up in irons, but at least you will be upright.
- If you really really have to fall in the water (missed straps, whatever), let go of the tiller extension but keep hold of the sheet. It will almost certainly capsize the boat, but at least you will not be separated from it or break the extension and end your race (which is what you'll achieve if you do it the other way round).
- If a lull/header is tipping you in to windward, remember that pulling yourself to the leeward side is effectively pulling the boat on top of you, exacerbating the problem. Instead, try getting the water to take your weight (helped by your buoyancy aid) relieving it from the hull. Easier to commit to in late summer than deep winter, this trick.
- Before righting, make sure the boat is actually right-able. Still-hoisted spinnakers, cleated mainsheets or over-tight kicking straps will all likely tip you in again straightaway. Sort them out first if you can.
- If the mast is pointed straight at the breeze, decide how you will deal with the likely capsize the other way. You can perhaps:
  - Sail her around.
  - Accept the inevitable and just go for the sprint through the boat to the other side.

- Show off with a San-Francisco-roll (stay on the plate and come out the other side – hold your breath!) Does not always work in very shallow water…

- Get the crew to hang on to the lower-side trapeze handle but be careful with this one – I have badly pranged a rib doing this, but it can be really effective in holding the righted boat stable.

- If you are going to make a habit of capsizes

  - Please make sure the buoyancy works in your boat (actually, do this regardless).

  - Investigate whether righting lines are permitted and useful in your class. They give you something to hang on to and can speed things up or even avoid a turtle.

Part 4
Making it Faster

Q: How the blazes do you go so fast?

A: Because, unlike you, I hike like ****

Q: *(to leading class sailmaker)* **– Why are my sails so slow?**

A: *(that he dare not give)* They are not.
The real issue is that you are *(to paraphrase)* a completely useless idiot

THREE-WEEK PROGRAMME
TO BETTER RESULTS

Considering how much we get out of our sailing, I find it amazing how little TLC many boats get. Is the ubiquity of fibreglass to blame? In the days of good old-fashioned tree wood, part of our sport was the fitting-out season, complete with wet-and-dry and the pervading smell of paint on a sunny spring day. Nowadays most of us do not even have an annual fitting-out hour. We might change a dodgy looking rope or fitting before it actually breaks but even that is not always the case. Doh! It broke. Off to the chandlers then.

As a result just taking the mould-covered cover off the boat can be a disgusting experience, a real disincentive to going sailing. Our kit is often seriously smelly and perhaps best described as 'tramp-chic'. The topsides are manky with decayed leaves, the undersides stained, chipped and probably covered in tape 'until I get to fix it properly' – which is likely to be sometime/later/never. Often the tidiest a boat ever becomes is when it is tarted-up for sale. How mad is that? We would not sort it out for ourselves, but we will for someone else?

Like almost anything else sails degrade over time. We wonder why we are going slowly when any objective appraisal would flag that a string vest is less porous than the rags we are trying to sail with.

Of course, there is always an exception: someone whose boat and kit are in wonderful order. They may be OCD types rather than talented sailors but they still have a significant edge over us Captain Slobs.

When I was a kid I raced Mirrors – boats made of iffy plywood – and sure enough, mid-season, the paint was cracking on mine. I turned up at an away regatta and proceeded to cover the undersides with Mr Sheen furniture polish. The objective was primarily to keep the water out of the cracks and improve what could otherwise be described as a crazy-paving finish. Inevitably the reception to this was universal leg-pulling, advice that matt finishes were better, wax was not the thing to use, blah blah blah.

As it happened, I won the Saturday race by a country mile. When I arrived on Sunday there were probably 20 Mirrors on their side being sprayed with furniture polish. Needless to say, it made no difference to anyone; the outcome was not dissimilar to the day before. The edge was still mine, they were putting their entire store in the wrong diagnosis.

It is time you got that furniture polish psychological edge for yourself. Time to give your sailing equipment some overdue TLC. Following this plan should help inspire you to sail more, go faster and increase your enjoyment when you do.

Week One – Evaluation

One night in the week:

- Find all your sailing gear

- Spread it out on the floor

- Put into two piles

    i. Rubbish that needs throwing away, is embarrassing or useless (buoyancy aids with no buoyancy left etc)

    ii. Perfectly usable (even if smelly!)

- Start a shopping list and write 'Mirazyme' on it – this is a miracle odour eliminator. Put ALL sailing kit in the bath, *just* cover with water, add Mirazyme, skoosh about then leave to soak overnight. Air dry and your kit will actually *not* smell. Oh it is such a relief! Vow to do this at least twice a year from now on.

2. At the next opportunity – it is boat check time. This is just to evaluate and prioritise what you need to do but take your sails, spares bag, a torch and toolbox anyway together with pen and notepad to make your shopping list.

    - First run eyes and hands **all** over the inside/topsides of the boat looking for cracks, loose, wobbly bits, bad chaffing (toe-straps!), fraying ropes etc and poorly functioning fittings. Do not forget self-bailers, transom flaps and buoyancy bungs. Imagine you are inspecting her with a view to buying.

    - Open hatch covers and shine the torch in. Is it dry in there? Do you see anything suspicious?

    - Also think back to when you last sailed. Does the board come up of its own volition? Does the rudder stay where it is supposed to be (down or up)? Does the rudder wobble in its fittings or tiller in the stock? What else was not quite right?

- If you have one of the rubber universal joints on your tiller extension check whether the rubber is failing. Disconnecting the extension from the tiller after sailing will increase the life of the joint dramatically.

- Write down everything that needs attention adding a big:

    i. *E* for Essential (iffy buoyancy, a line about to break)

    ii. *P* for Preventative – the cause of a chaffed rope, a scratch needing attention

    iii. *C* for Cosmetic

- Measure any ropes that were in the **E** category – note the function and length on your shopping list. If replacing control lines think about making them continuous. To do so you will need the splicing tools, some practice and longer ropes but it is really cool if you can – look on YouTube for some how-to videos.

- I suggest the default position is that any shockcord ought to be replaced, you may not realise how far gone it was until you replace it with new.

- Now cast a sharp eye over the spars and rigging and note any issues such as sticking sheaves.

- Sails – before hauling them up, lay them out and give them a good check over for breaking stitching, dodgy batten pockets, missing tell-tales and the like. Note any issues then pull the sails up and appraise them. Are they still looking sharp or best sent to the scrapheap?

- Undersides – when did you last have a good look? (Capsizes do not count!). If you can roll her over – otherwise lay the cover on the ground (outside down!) and crawl under for a good look with that torch. Look really closely at slot gaskets and bailers but also for cracks and scratches. Knackered slot gaskets probably slow a boat more than anything else. Again, jot down your findings.

- While you are there inspect the trolley – is it supporting the boat properly? Are chocks that should move now rusted solid? Has the padding disappeared? Is there any air in the tyres?

3. On the next club sailing day, go out of your way to have a look at other similar boats and compare their systems etc with your own. Also have a chat with the fleet leaders, perhaps show them your boat and pick their brains as to what they would prioritise. The objective here is to avoid replacing like with like if there is a better way.

4. You might also want to see what boat-bimbling tips appear on your boat's Class Association website. Having done all this, price up your shopping list – but **do not** go shopping until you have undertaken the next step.

5. Now is the time for a cold, hard evaluation. Think about what needs doing on the boat, the state of the sails and everything else, consider whether it is worth the cost, time and effort to fix or whether to trade up to a replacement. Have a browse on Apollo Duck, Yachts and Yachting and the Class Association website and see what is available and at what cost – you may be pleasantly surprised. It might even be time to expand your horizons and try your hand at something else – a change is as good as a rest and all that. Sorry if I have created some inner turmoil! Do not be put off though: if it is going to be a keeper, think like Bob-the-Builder. Can we fix it? Yes we can! (Probably)

6. Now it is shopping time. You can shop online, or by visiting your local chandler, for the bits you have identified plus, if you do not have them already:

   - O-ring seals for inspection hatches (if you have that type)
   - A dry (non-oil based) lubricating spray such as McLube (from the chandler)
   - A marine cleaner like Muc-Off Boat Cleaner
   - Plastic (electrical) tape
   - A lighter for sealing rope ends
   - T-Cut or a similar cutting polish

- WD40
- A permanent marker pen
- Waterproof notebook
- A spare buoyancy bung. Keep it in your kitbag – you will thank me one day for this tip.

If in doubt go to a chandler or pick up the phone for a chat rather than guess.

7. Also find a bucket, scrubbing brush and retired toothbrush (for attacking corners and inaccessible places).

Week two – TLC time

1. Now for some effort. Strip all the ropes out of the boat and take out the mast.

2. Mast and boom:

   • Take off any tape around spreaders or elsewhere.

   • Give them a good wash down to get rid of mould and birdlime. If the masthead has been stuck in the mud, run a hose down the inside to clean it out.

   • When dry, re-wrap the spreader fittings with new plastic tape. Use a knife or scissors to cut the tape, rather than tear it. The end will stay sealed for far longer that way.

   • Ensure all blocks are free from dirt and running smoothly – give them a squirt of PTFE lubricating spray (but definitely **not** WD40).

   • If you use a rope main halyard, take a couple of inches off the top to more the wear-point before it fails.

   • While the boat is off the trolley, spray any stuck trolley parts with WD40 until they are moving again. Give the axles a squirt of silicon lube. Also write your name and sail number in several obvious places on the trolley. Pump up the tyres.

3. Undersides:

   • Turn her upside down (resting on some grass or padding) and give that underside a good clean up. Wash down with Muc-Off or a domestic cleaner then allow to dry. If still looking stained, it is time for that T-Cut and some elbow grease.

   • If any scratches go through the gelcoat or through the paint down to the wood, they will need sealing as appropriate if not now, then soon.

   • Change the slot gasket if it has gone. You will find some tips for this job from Pete Vincent on the RS Class Association web site here: *www.rs-association.com/index.asp/ fleet=RS400&selection=Technical%20Details&marker=240* or ask a professional like Pete to do it for you.

   • According to Frank Bethwaite's hugely well-researched but

'challenging' book, the most important part of a dinghy to have a mirror-like finish is the foils, so give these a good going over – certainly do not forget them. Another time, you may want to fill scratches, chips and dents, repaint them and rub down with ever-finer wet-and-dry on a sanding block (up to 1500-2000 grit) then use cutting polish until they have a mirror finish. Or not. I have heard the counter-argument that the plate needs a good, grippy non-slip finish – because you won't then slide off when standing on it. I *think* this comment was ironic.

4. Cockpit and topsides:

    - Give everything a spray with Muc-Off and whatever else it takes to make it clean and shiny. You will be amazed at the psychological lift this will give you on the water.

    - Wash, clean and free-up all blocks, cam-cleats and other moving parts, then spray with lube until good as new (or change them if completely worn out). Do not forget the self-bailers.

    - Replace those dodgy ropes and shockcord, making sure ends are sealed with a cigarette lighter (but please do not burn your fingers like I always do)

    - If in doubt, leave lines a bit too long rather than find you have cut them too short. Tie a bowline rather than a stopper knot in the ends perhaps.

    - Change those hatch-cover seals.

    - Anything that can snag and rip a spinnaker will. So if you sail a boat with a kite, re-tape any split rings, pins or other kite-rippers

    - For now, cover any holes in the gelcoat with plastic tape – but fix properly as soon as you can.

5. Cover:

   - These can go disgustingly mouldy over time. Jet-washing sounds appealing but in my experience it either does not do the job or it blasts holes through the canvas. So, out with the scrubbing brush.

6. Reassemble.

Week three - Longer–term jobs
Patch gelcoat and paintwork chips – choose a fine day to do this.

1. Fill, sand and re-spray foils *www.youtube.com/watch?v=nqDHK0VcKTE*

2. Eye splices *www.youtube.com/watch?v=MTJSLVQhjB4*

3. Taper sheets *www.youtube.com/watch?v=7bWZpUQZO8E*

4. Make control lines continuous *www.youtube.com/watch?v=4LbX7jLGkYM*

TOOLS, TRICKS AND GADGETS

Stopwatch
Perhaps the best £9.99 you will spend. Get something waterproof with a countdown function you can reset for three or five minute start sequences. If you want to spend more, there is lots of choice but leave the Swiss-made family heirloom at home. Without a watch, realistically you cannot start well. You cannot win the race at the start, but you can lose it.

Burgee
You need one. At the top of the mast, not at eye-level. Burgees are crucial inland where the wind at the top of the rig can be dramatically different from that at deck level.

Tell-tales
Three sets for jib and main, evenly spaced up the sail, 25% back from the leading edge. Add one ribbon on the leech at the top batten height. Suddenly, you stand a chance of knowing how the air is flowing across the sail.

A length of 2mm vectran rope
My brother's favourite. Keep it in your buoyancy aid. Amazingly strong, in an emergency it will cover for exploded shackles, jury-rig ripped toe-straps or replace, say a Laser traveller line. Taylor the length to what you think it might need cover for. Even better, splice a loop into one end too. If you've borrowed a boat, take two pieces!

Compasses
Are compasses for the club sailor? Perhaps not. They are certainly unnecessary for most harbours and puddles but for open water I do like my Tacktick electronic compass. The Laser class bans electronics, so a traditional magnetic is the only option.

Some caveats about compasses. First choose your day carefully; on some days they are useful (those regular tick-tock oscillations) and on others they can be misleading, for example when the wind is progressively swinging one way or there is a geographical wind-bend. Second, they are a distraction from having your head out of the boat and being aware of what is going on around you, which is often more important. Third, particularly with strong tides around, windshifts are not always the priority.

Top tip: when not in use, keep your Tacktick in direct sunlight or under a daylight bulb to keep it charged, but don't leave it on a home on a day you will need it.

Sadly, a compass is like a stills-camera: it only gives you a snapshot of what is happening in that instant. They rely on your memory to retain how readings are changing over time. To monitor changes over time we need...

Waterproof paper and a pencil
Waterproof paper pads are widely available from good chandlers. Tape a sheet or two to the boat somewhere easily visible. Tie a pencil into the boat nearby (sharpen both ends) – I hold mine in place with Velcro. Now you can keep notes of wind headings over time and give yourself a chance to see the bigger picture. It may sound a bit too organised and professional – but is not hard, so try it; sometimes it will be like removing a blindfold.

Final thought on this topic – as you note bearings, also look upwards (and upwind) for any clouds – after all, clouds can have rather a significant impact on the breeze. Putting it another way, the timing of shifts may be random in absolute time terms, but if it is always X minutes before the next cloud passes over the course, *that* is seriously useful information.

Waterproof paper has another use of course – you can map where racing marks are and note down the course, lap numbers etc. If you do multiple laps and lose count like I do, mark off each lap like a prisoner counting down the days (sorry about the analogy). It is amazing how often even the top guys lose count of the number of laps.

Laminators
If you have access to a laminator, a whole new world of fun opens up. Checklists, maps, tidal atlases, course lists and more can be laminated and taped onto, or stored in, the boat. If you have a beautiful, wooden ship, however, be warned that blanking off a rectangle of varnished surface for a season could create a colour mismatch afterwards.

Lubber-lines
Do you have trouble judging lay-lines, particularly downwind in an asymmetric? A couple of sighting lines angled across your foredeck in tape or Magic Marker (easily removed with solvent) are all you need. Calibrate them for a medium breeze and remember that your angles will be a bit deeper when windy, and hotter when lighter.

Glasses retainers

If, like me, you wear prescription specs but cannot wear contact lenses, get some retainers to keep your glasses on your head and use an old pair for sailing rather than go without. I find I am noticeably slower without my glasses. Also good for sunnies.

Hats

I will often put a hat in the boat. During a race, it will only get near my head to keep rain off my glasses or if it is brain-freezingly cold. The rationale? Bare heads are excellent weather vanes, extremely sensitive to variations in the breeze. When not racing, the sun-protection or heat-retention is welcome, so out comes the hat.

Part 5
Speed

Boatspeed makes you a tactical genius

Marketing strapline of a leading sailmaker

The trouble with good boatspeed is that, if you go the wrong way, it's a lot further to come back

Paul Elvstrøm (greatest dinghy sailor ever)

THE ESSENTIAL FIVE-ESSENTIALS

Despite all the effort you may put in to applying the guidance above you may still be held back by not having any real boatspeed relative to your competitors. A lack of boatspeed tends to manifest itself by just about holding on to the fleet when you get the tactics spot on but otherwise inexorably dropping backwards.

Now most of us club sailors become a bit blasé about the RYA's five essentials, thinking they are a learning phase we go through at the outset of our sailing life but can later forget. Please think again. For most club sailors, there is an excellent chance that if they just revisit (and apply perfectly) those five essentials, their boatspeed will improve noticeably. To remind you, they are:

- Sail trim

- Course sailed

- Balance .

- Centreboard

- Trim

So let's reprise them in a buit more detail.

Sail Trim

We all know that the wind is never constant in strength or direction, and that it differs again as you move up the rig. Therefore if you are not constantly assessing (and probably adjusting) sail trim you are not putting in enough effort. Tell-tales are of course essential because they are so much more sensitive than the crude measure of the sail flapping. With two or three sails set, is everything moving in unison or is one sail neglected and adversely impacting another (such as through a choked slot)? If your crew is not constantly playing the jib on a two-sail reach, you need them to understand that this is their opportunity to make a real difference with skill rather than just as sack-of-meat ballast. This may be a topic for discussion off the water, but if you have agreed goals and ambitions, no helm should feel guilty about encouraging the crew to do their job properly. It is a race not a cruise after all.

Even upwind, it is rarely a case a case of jam the jib-sheet and forget about it until the next tack. Humans are not programmed to look up, which is not helpful. If we were everyone would know how hyper-critical jib-sheet tension is. A lull or 5mm too much sheet can change a jib-main slot from perfect to air-brakingly choked.

To demonstrate this put your boat on the beach, in clear wind, sails up, sheets-in. Together with the crew have a play to see just how sensitive that slot is to a few millimetres of sheet tension (please do not let the boat blow over!). Marking the sheets at a good average position is a start – plastic tape (to the outside of the fairlead) will usually do the job. Referring the crew to the slot width (say at spreader height) rather than saying "Ease 5mm of sheet" will help them to look in the right place, understand what you want and help you achieve it.

Course Sailed
Re-read the sections above about downwind sailing.

Upwind, some people really struggle to concentrate or multi-task sufficiently to keep the tell-tales streaming exactly at all times. Often I see lengths and lengths thrown away by sailing too low or missing a big lift. The outcome may feel like poor speed – in actual fact the problem is with the nut on the tiller.

Balance
Flat.
Flatter.
No. Really flat.
Come on. That's only not quite flat!
We want flaaaat.

Am I setting myself up to be called a hypocrite here?

Only two exceptions. One: a ballasted keel boat. Two: it is a ghosting day.

If your boat has chines, look behind you. If there are swirls off just the leeward transom quarter, you are dipping that corner and are not flat. Not fast.

Which lead us to how. Upwind, there are two ways. One is to pinch a bit, 'feathering' the sails. The other is to ease the sails, particularly the main. Yes, you can combine the two. Remember that although the sail will lift more, losing power, the resultant driving force will also be more forwards and less sideways. The latter reduces the heeling moment. The former pushes you forwards more. In a big gust, I will not hesitate to have my boom three or four feet from the transom quarter to stay flat. This all assumes you have pulled the kicker and cunningham on tight enough; don't be gentle with them, they need to be on harder than most people will credit.

Downwind, the options are slightly different. You could ease the sail (and kicker, the resulting twist sheds power from the top) but better, bear away and bank the gain to leeward, allowing you to point higher and so go faster when the gust has past. A win-win.

If you were caught out and a gust does heel the boat, do not be shy about using your weight. When it's windy, an aggressive bounce can make all the difference between getting back flat then shooting off or heeling, dipping the boom in the water, broaching and perhaps falling in.

Centreboard

Generally, everyone is pretty good with moving foils about, although I found asymmetric sailing made me lazy. As the plate usually stays down with the kite up (pulling it up creates lee-helm) I discovered I was not pulling it up on non-kite off-wind legs. Doing so helps the boat feel nicer and is quicker.

If you have a daggerboard boat and can lift it downwind, put a Magic Marker line across it so that, when pulled up to the line, the board **just** closes off the case like a plug. Withdraw any more and you'll leave all sorts of turbulence in the case that slows you down unnecessarily.

Trim

Fore and aft weight positioning.
Our natural tendency is to sit too far aft. In average conditions, the knuckle of the bow should, as a minimum, just be in the water. Try sliding forward a bit and listen to whether the wake sounds cleaner. In some boats, you can of course look too. Observe where the crew sits. Many crews hold a mistaken belief that thwarts are provided for them to sit on, whereas we know they are actually there solely to brace the centreboard case and keep the sides of the boat apart. If crews sit on 'the seat' they may well be far farther aft than they would be if they were sitting out. Is it coincidence that the crew's end is more cramped, uncomfortable and criss-crossed with rope and wire than the helms, when helms tend to be the boat-owner? Unlikely. Comfort just is

not in the crew's job description. So either the crew needs to move forward or the helm needs to get in front of that crossbeam. If you then leave your mainsheet in their way (as I usually do) ready to tangle them up during roll-tacks, they may take the hint and move forwards themselves!

Some rules of thumb: in a Laser, the front leg should be right at the front of the cockpit. In an Enterprise, the crew should gain a dent up their forward side where the helm squeezes them into the shroud. If I recall, in a 470, any rising bow-wave should hit the trapezing crew's feet and deflect into the helm's face as soon as they stop hiking hard. Good design feature, that. Soaking downwind in a 200, the crew should be kneeling, one leg each side of the plate case, right up against the bulkhead. If it were meant to be comfortable, armchairs would be on the options list! In chop or waves, they will probably need to move back a bit of course.

This is all fine for an average breeze, when you are displacement sailing and speed is a function of waterline length. If it is ghosting-along light, the principles change: the primary constraint on speed for any wind-speed becomes drag from the wetted surface area. Which is why we get even further forward (foredeck for skiff crews) and heel a bit to get the flat planing sections of the hull out of the water. Immersing the narrow curvy bits at the front is a price well worth paying to get the wide stern sections out.

When it comes to planing time, generally everyone tends to move back, as they should – although not always far enough, in a Laser particularly. What is less likely to happen is the return forward to normal displacement-sailing position as you come off the plane. Does this sound like you?

BOAT TUNE

There are hugely technical tomes out there on boat tune; but we club sailors need to see the wood for the trees.

Has any one else noticed that Formula One motor racing these days seems to be 90% about aerodynamics rather than the dirty, oily bits? Of course our aerodynamics are far more complicated than theirs but ultimately it still comes down to balance, power management and drag.

Balance

This is relatively simple – when we have the five essentials all spot on, we want the rudder blade to be exactly central and the boat to track in a straight line. Too much sideways push in front of the plate and we will have lee-helm, so need to pull the tiller to windward to track straight and vice versa.

Most classes or sailmakers have tuning sheets that give settings for mast step position and rake to help achieve this. Not many one-designs allow you to move the whole plate fore and aft in the boat although in theory that is an alternative. What you should not do is rake the plate fore or aft to achieve helm balance upwind. All the science indicates that the leading edge of the plate should be vertical.

Power management

In a perfect world, our mast/sail combination would be so clever that, once the rig is fully powered up for our weight and personal righting efforts, it would flex automatically to shed any excess. But that would be boring. Modern flexible rigs do indeed act as shock absorbers, making an effort in that regard, yet they are well away from the theoretical ideal.

In the same way that those F1 cars want maximum down-force in the corners but far less on the straights, we want all the power we can get from our rig right up to the point where we cannot cope with any more. After that we want to lose further power **without creating drag**, just like those F1 cars on the straight. Drag, after all slows us down.

Until the advent of their Drag Reduction System (DRS) in 2011, F1 cars were stuck with a fixed aerofoil section for their downforce. Even now the adjustment is pretty crude. I am going to swap metaphors now, with our control lines, we can change the shape of the whole section, effectively converting our rig from a rounded, slow, heavy-lifting Hercules transporter plane wing to a thin, slippery Concorde one. Genius. If we pull the right strings and the mast/sail makers did their job, that is.

Continuing the aeroplane metaphor, remember that increasing mast rake is used to shed power on a sailboat (I am not clever enough to explain why, but I know it works) in the same way Concorde or an F1-11 have swept back wings and a Hercules does not.

So how do we use our controls to shed power when we have enough? With increased rake (if you can) – easy on a Phantom, less so on a Laser. Applying kicker bends the mast, both by pulling the top back as well as thrusting the boom forward into the mast (assuming we let off the restraints to low down mast bend (struts, rams, lowers etc). Effectively the sailcloth becomes spread over a wider area, making it flatter. Unfortunately all that leech tension has the effect of pulling the point of maximum depth in the sail towards the trailing edge, exactly where we do not want it to be for a low drag shape. Luckily Mr Cunningham had a remedy for that, pulling it back forwards and incidentally opening the leech at the top, reducing drag further. Clever chap, Mr C. I'd hazard a guess that most club sailors don't pull the kicker on hard enough once over-powered. Fewer still will pull on sufficient sneaky-pig (cunning-ham, geddit?). Most people's end point should be their start-point. Get pulling – you may find it to be a revelation.

To many, spreaders are a complete mystery but all they do is allow you to tune the mast to your particular righting moment, making the mast more or less gust-responsive (forward stiffens fore and aft, out stiffens sideways). Unless you are significantly heavier or lighter than average, I would suggest using the sailmakers recommended settings and not worry about them further.

With increased wind-speed, as more air flows over the jib it may struggle to get through that small gap between jib and main, so pulling fairleads back frees up the jib leech and gives the air more of a chance.

If only it were that simple. In fact it is far more difficult. Armed with this theoretical knowledge we club sailors need a couple of things. First, the awareness to recognise when the wind has changed significantly and to respond by adjusting our controls accordingly. Second, the understanding that, while we could spend the whole race with our focus inside the boat, doing so is not conducive to winning because we will miss windshifts, laylines and more besides.

If we were truly serious, we would go out two-boat tuning with someone on a par with ourselves then test and log every optimal setting in every condition and log everything after every race too. But we are not. So the best compromise is to glean what we can from sail-makers' tuning sheets, settings posted on class websites and any nuggets we can pick up from the club hotshots. Then just get sailing.

Thereafter it is worth trying to take a mental snapshot of the rig when the boat feels as though it is going particularly nicely, to build a visual databank over time.

If we think back to our five essentials we will recall that, when close-hauled, we get lots of sideways push from the rig and not much forward. Then as we progressively bear off, we get less sideways force and more forwards – so for the same righting moment we can handle more power, which is why we go faster on a reach. We may still need to depower; just be wary of excess kicker. When the boom is a long way out, a gust can drag it in the water if we heel. Hence it is safer to depower with twist. With kicker eased there is far less nasty drag than if we tried this approach on a beat.

Spinnakers
The biggest boo-boos I see on club spinnakers are poles being too high, so the sail will not fill, or too low, choking the luff. Clews want to be close as possible to level. After that it is all about trimming, concentration and keeping the pole as far back as possible while keeping the sail off the forestay – the pole angled as an extension to the main-boom is a good guide.

Asymmetrics
In heat-up mode, treat them like a big jib. Pretty straight-forward but in waves be ready to sheet on as you accelerate down a wave as the apparent wind swings forwards then ease as you climb up the next wave face and the apparent reverts aft.

Asymmetric soak-mode is the hardest sail trimming to do well in a dinghy. If the kite starts collapsing from the leech, the sheet needs to ease and the helm head up, as you are sailing too low. The danger is that crews sheet on when it starts to fold, making it worse. Talk to each other, look behind to see the gusts and lulls coming and keep the thing filling at all costs. A bit of windward heel may pull it out from behind the mainsail's wind-shadow, but do not overdo it.

The biggest enemy of good light-air kite trimming is a heavy, water-absorbing sheet. Sail with sheets as thin and light as you dare. Better yet taper the business end too.

MASTERING WEIRD WIND EFFECTS

Wind – pretty essential to what we do, huh? In this section we will consider some subtleties you may not have thought of. Master them and you could make some nice gains.

Apparent versus true

Everyone understands about apparent wind, even if subconsciously. Stick your hand out of a moving car window on a windless day and you will feel a big breeze – that's apparent wind – generated by the vehicle's movement through the air, rather than the air's own movement. We deal with this effect all the time when sailing but tend not to think about it – but we should.

Upwind, it is changes in wind-speed that have the most impact – although the effect can take on a disguise. Imagine you are sailing close-hauled in a moderate breeze when all of a sudden the wind completely disappears. Your boat will still maintain some momentum – but as you are now moving through still air, you are effectively head-to-wind. The boat will act in precisely the same way as if you had hit a 45-degree header. In a more real-world scenario, where the wind lulls from, say, eight mph to five mph (direction remaining constant) a similar but less extreme effect takes place. It feels as though you have been headed – tell-tales lift and sails even back. **Do not be fooled** into tacking. If you do, you will experience the dreadful feeling that has made us all groan so many times in the past – that of turning the boat seemingly forever before the sails will fill on the other side.

Technically this is known as a velocity-sheer. In future, when it feels like a header but it is also a lull, just wait a second rather than rolling straight into a tack. Adjust to get the boat upright again of course, but a big bear away will just lose you distance to windward with from the braking effect of the rudder, slowing you to no benefit. If it really is only a wind-speed issue, things will normalise in a moment. So hang on in there and let it settle so you can make an informed decision what to do next.

Of course sometimes you can see these coming and be ready to react.

Conversely, as a gust hits, you can get the opposite effect, particularly in heavy or under-canvassed boats. The apparent wind effect is reduced by an increase in windspeed, giving the appearance of a lift until a new equilibrium is reached, at which point the short-lived 'lift' will end, resulting in what appears to be a small header. Again it may well not be, so let things settle and do not be misled into tacking.

Sailing into the wind also speeds up the frequency with which you encounter windshifts. Running downwind is the opposite – sailing away from the breeze reduces the frequency with which you encounter windshifts. So if there are typically four shifts on your beat, you might only get one or two on a run so it is even more important to get them right.

While close-hauled sailing also by definition creates apparent windspeed, running does the opposite. When you add to that the danger of air not flowing cleanly around the sails (instead pushing one side and creating turbulent stalled air on the other) it is no real surprise that dead-running can be horribly slow. Therefore in virtually every class it pays to create a bit of angle to ensure there is some decent airflow across the rig. How much depends on the boat and wind strength – to find the sweet spot, watch your class hotshots and do not be afraid to try heading up more than you have in the past.

With unstayed masts as on a Laser, it is often faster to sail a run by the lee, with the airflow reversed, so it rolls from leech to luff, with the tell-tales pointing at the mast. Weird but true. Just do not let the boom out beyond perpendicular.

The whole business of running before the wind has become an irrelevance in many modern classes. Asymmetric spinnakers and hydrofoils create a virtuous circle – heading up increases power and so speed, increasing apparent wind, which creates more power and so on. Get this right and you can find yourself going faster *and* lower than other boats that rounded, hoisted and pointed passively towards the mark. As a result it is often possible to gain more downwind in these classes than upwind.

Wind variations up the rig

In Frank Bethwaite's 'magnum opus' textbook High Performance Sailing he reports some experiments on variations in wind speed at different heights up the rig. To summarise, friction between air and water slows the wind at surface level but this effect dissipates a few feet up. Those of us sailing inland and in estuaries also experience wind-shadows from trees and hills that exacerbate the situation. However, even in open water in light breezes the effect is most pronounced – you could have 2mph at water level and 6mph at the top of the rig. Which brings us back to apparent wind. If this is driving the boat at say 1 mph, at deck level the sails may need to be set as if close-hauled even on a reach – whereas at the top of the rig, the apparent wind effect is far less so the sails may need to be sheeted at a far broader angle. This leads to the conclusion that in light airs it could be hugely faster to sail with a quite exaggerated amount of twist – so negligible vang and jib leads right back. The feedback is all there in the tell-tales – but sometimes we need a scientific explanation to rationalise the evidence of our eyes. So here you go; twist can be really fast.

Downdrafts

The wind does not always blow horizontally, thankfully, or some of us would never get any! Often gusts blow downwards, sometimes at quite a steep angle, again particularly inland and on estuaries. As this moving air hits the water it spreads out in perhaps a semi-circle from the impact point. To demonstrate this effect hold your hand out flat and horizontal, fingers together, then move it downwards whilst splaying your fingers out.

Sailing upwind, this can have a devastating impact. As you reach one gust cell, first you get headed – perhaps 20 or 30 degrees. Then almost straightaway you get lifted and lifted and lifted and lifted, well above the direction you were going before the header. This feels fantastic at the time but the next gust cell is approaching rapidly and now you are pointing well above the mean wind direction, perhaps by 35-40 degrees. The first part of that next gust cell will now present itself as a huge header of more than 45 degrees. This spells big trouble – as you are likely sitting out hard in a gust and the sails are about to fill on the opposite side. Uh-oh. Splash.

And that is why I used to keep capsizing to windward.

All this technical insight is good to know, but what can you **do** about it? First, be aware it is coming, so prepared. Second, rather than head up and bear-off so dramatically in each cell, sail a more average course, ease the sails in the lift, stay flat and go for speed instead. Third, be ready to move fast, even if this means not sitting out to the ultimate (but keep the boat upright of course). Fourth, particularly in the likes of a Laser with its low freeboard, sometimes you can let the water take your body-weight, aided by the buoyancy in your lifejacket, and relieve the windward heeling force that way. Don't forget, though, that grabbing the far toe strap or gunwale is actually pulling the boat over on top of you!

If the gust cells are sufficiently far apart, another trick is to have the centre of each past behind you. If it looks like it will pass in front, tack, so it will then pass behind. This tactic will keep you on the lifted tack.

Updrafts

Conversely, the wind also gets forced upwards. This is particularly relevant in two situations. Firstly on reservoirs, where wind flows up a dam wall and keeps going, creating a wind-shadow near the windward shore, before gravity reasserts itself. Secondly under leeward-shore cliffs where all sorts of weird things can happen, depending on the specific topography. Thankfully, avoiding leeward shore cliffs is in most sailors' DNA.

RUDDER: FRIEND OR FOE?

Answer: a foe, pretending to be a (fair-weather) friend.

Boats with tiny or crazily-shaped blades will virtually always let you down. A boat with a decent rudder design may indeed get you out of trouble sometimes but there is always a heavy price to pay. At best, rudder equals brake. At worst that crash or capsize still ensues.

Despite the way it may often feel, your boat does not really have a mind of its own. It just responds to the forces of weight, wind and water acting upon it. So it is up to you to make use of *all* the controls at your disposal to make the boat change direction, with the rudder the device of lowest priority.

It may be a long time since you went for a rudderless sail, so perhaps it's time to have another go. Or with a single-hander, tie the tiller to the centreline with shockcord (with a quick release knot in case of emergencies). Either way go for only half centreboard or you may just end up dizzy.

There are two main routes to rudderless steering.

1. Heel:

    i.   Leeward heel makes the boat head-up.

    ii. Windward heel makes the boat bear away.

2. Sail trim:

    i.   Mainsail-out bears away, helping the boat heel to windward by reducing heeling forces.

    ii. Mainsail-in heads you up, helping the boat heel to leeward by increasing heeling forces.

    iii. Foresail-in bears away, foresail-out and you head up, with similar but lesser heeling impact to the mainsail.

It is now time to put these tips to good use. At every change of direction, aim to get into the habit of using these actions, rather than the rudder, as the primary driver. Let the rudder blade be the follower, not the leader. Perhaps the fact it lives at the back of the boat is a clue to how it should be used?

For significant changes of direction, such as mark roundings, think about the sail controls too. With many boats if the kicking strap is still maxed-on at the windward mark, easing the mainsheet will not be enough. The over-tight leech will keep the sail powered up regardless, so the boat refuses to make the turn. Hence, it is essential to ease the kicker sufficiently in advance too if you want the big bear-away to happen.

Part 6
Wise Words

Few of the many wise apothegms which have been uttered have prevented a
single foolish action
Thomas B. Macauley

Honesty is the first chapter in the book of wisdom
Thomas Jefferson

It is much more difficult to measure nonperformance than performance
Harold S Geneen

TEN COMMANDMENTS

1. Prioritise and adapt.

2. Do not mix 'jobs for body' and 'jobs for brain'.

3. Join in at the start.

4. Keep your head out of the boat.

5. Keep doing the right thing, going the right way. Be positive, always.

   It is a 470 qualifier at Rutland, there is a grant to represent the country at Cannes riding on the combined result of this and another meeting at Grafham (of which more later). We have been chasing our rivals for second place for the whole darn (windy) race but whatever we do, we cannot get close enough to get a lock on them. As I drop the kite for the final time, I go into 'bonkers-mode', singing happily at the top of my voice ('Alice's Restaurant' if you need this trick yourself) as they pass going upwind. But, wahoo, we pip them in the last few yards.

   Later, I find myself standing in the shower next to guess who? Gentlemanly as ever, I apologise for sneaking past them at the death. "That's OK," he says in return, continuing, "We knew you were going to get us, you just sounded so cheerful."

6. Keep going until the finish line is crossed - be relentless. Do not choke. You have been better than Joe Bloggs for x minutes why should that change suddenly after x+1 minutes?

7. Inject intensity bursts at pinch points such as starts, mark roundings and the finish line.

8. Keep the boat moving – be where the breeze is.

9. Keep the boat flat flat flat.

10. Get the five essentials right, every second.

A DOZEN FAVOURITE SCHOOLBOY ERRORS

1. Being late for the start.

2. Not knowing the course, rounding marks the wrong way, misunderstanding start and finish lines and shortening course communication.

   There we are - last race of that combined 470 qualifier at Grafham. We have had a good weekend again so far but cannot afford a discard. We are well placed at the first mark in only a light breeze. Pull! It is a great hoist, kite snaps full and we are off, except...why is the boat heeling? Ah! Helm has decided that now is the time to fall on to his back and show off his dying-fly impression. So I'm out on the wire and dump the kite but no good, over we go and the whole fleet sails past, proffering 'useful' advice, while we sort ourselves out. Grrrr. To add insult to this particular injury, the wind changes so the course now comprises a run, fetch and reach for 90 minutes. How can you come back in a soldier's race? We cannot.

   But wait a minute, 20 yards beyond what should be the weather mark is a committee boat with some interestingly blue-themed flags hoisted. No one else has spotted this – they are all sailing away, kites up. Nonchalantly (OK, sneakily) assuming the air of 'Give this one up for a bad job' we sail on, cross the line to a loud cannon and a race win. Did we laugh at the ensuing chaos? Yeah, baby.

3. Getting the tide wrong.

4. Low blood sugar/dehydration/sunburn.

5. Wrong clothes, being too hot or, worse, too cold.

   Arguably not friendly, but it works; when sailing up and down waiting for the umpteenth post-general recall start sequence to start, I spotted someone shivering. "Cor, you look cold" I said sympathetically. Suddenly, I felt warmer. Tried it on someone else. Same again. And again. Evil but effective.

6. Not racing the fleet.

7. Fliers. Desperately sad.

8. Gear failure.

9. Crashes and doing 720s.

10. Avoidable swims and capsizes.

11. Not signing on or off and forgetting tallies.

12. Over-standing marks.

VENTURING FORTH

In my experience, finding the road trailer, light-board et al and venturing forth occasionally truly helps your club-sailing performance. Apart from anything else, it shakes you out of entrenched habits and makes you think. To this end I suggest going somewhere dissimilar rather than a home-club-clone. As a puddle sailor, I try and go for the contrast of open water, preferably the uppy-downy salty stuff, at least until I get there and it is blowing 25 knots minimum!

To make the most of the trip, it is worth doing a bit of planning. Arriving late and stressed is not generally conducive to enhanced performance. So know where you are going. Google Maps and even Google Street View should enable you to find the club. Driving 95% of the way around, say, Rutland Water, looking for the club entrance is not recommended. If you have booked accommodation for a two-day event, make sure you know where that is too.

Check out weather and tides. See if you can find a venue guide. If you are going somewhere like Chichester Harbour with myriad randomly-named marks, download and laminate (or cling film might do) a harbour map from the club website and stick it on the boat. If you're going somewhere obscure make sure you have enough cash and even a good old-fashioned cheque for the entry fee. For an Open, I tend to avoid entering in advance and online – if there is too much or too little wind for my taste, I might wimp out when I get there, so I'd rather pay when I am ready.

Write yourself a list of stuff to take – which should always include your spares box, compass/Tacktick (fully charged already of course) trailer spare wheel and the right size spanner or wheel brace. Murphy's Law says that if you forget either of these you will definitely need them. Take snacks and drinks bottles for on the water unless you are 100% confident you can buy what you need at the host club. If camping, remember to take a pillow (well I always forget mine) and pitch away from the notorious snorers.

Experience has taught me not to leave packing the boat up until the day of the event, no matter how close the venue and how late the start. Do this in advance and you will be much more relaxed on the day.

When you get there find somewhere sensible to park the boat so that others do not hold you up when you want to launch. Always attend the briefing. Make sure you know where the marks are. Read the race instructions carefully. Never assume you know what they say – you will be wrong. Find out how long it will take to get to the starting area, at Frensham that is not a hard calculation but fighting the tide in Fowey Harbour before the breeze arrives can take an age. Do not be late – aim to be ready to launch as soon as the briefing is over.

Introduce yourself to the people around you in the boat park and lunch queue. Be friendly; remember you are an ambassador for your club and it would be great to encourage some of these people to come to your club open meeting. Before launching, put your valuables, including car key, somewhere secure.

Once on the water, get busy immediately. Think about how the landscape will impact the breeze, both as it is now and how it is forecast to be. Is a sea breeze likely to appear or will a weather front radically change things? Get a feel for the chop/waves, upwind and down. Hoist the kite to check it is rigged properly. Get some gybes in. Do you really want the first of the day to be a high-pressured one? On open water, log the wind bearing every few minutes as described earlier. Establish those start-line transits but keep an eye out for the OOD moving one end of the line.

Establish your race strategy and plan your start accordingly. Tactics will need adapting too, compared with at your home club. Laylines and marks could be far more crowded than for club-races. Plan your approach accordingly, which is likely to mean being more conservative.

After race one, get yourself refuelled and ponder what went right and wrong. Do not be despondent if it felt like a disaster.

Our first ever RS200 Open was at Littleton and there was a huge turnout for such a small gravel pit. I sailed like an idiot and we were pretty much last in the first race to the extent that we decided we preferred a DNF to the placing so we missed the finish line on purpose. Next race was average at best and over lunch serious navel-gazing took place. It worked; we won the next race comfortably before reverting to near Averageville in the last.

So do not give up. Every dog has its day!

WORDS OF WISDOM

Paul Elvstrøm*
- You have not won the race if, in winning, you lose the respect of your competitors.

- Good competition is more important than speed. (For a class to be successful).

- Keelboats are for elderly people. (Said when aged 70).

- Always seek a position from which winning is possible, not one from which winning is impossible.

- The trouble with good boatspeed is that, if you go the wrong way, it is a lot further to come back.

Dr Stuart Walker
- Cross them when you can.

- Do not let them cross you.

- Spend a lead to save a lead.

- Take the long tack (or gybe) first.

- Keep closer to the rhumb line than your competitor. (I would caveat that with unless it is a really light airs day).

Roger Gilbert
- Success is three things. Getting there. Staying there. Doing it consistently. (Easy for him to say).

- In response to the question 'how do I point higher?' the answer was 'get a longer tiller extension' followed, to be fair, with a tour de force rationalisation.

Uffa Fox
- Weight is only useful in a steamroller. Mind you he also reckoned that a Dragon would always be cheap to buy and run.

Rusty Eplett (yes, my Dad)
- I can teach you to sail in an hour, but one lifetime is not long enough to truly master it.

- To me (when I was aged 25): "I have forgotten more about sailing than you know." Me: "But you have never even been to a Nationals* - I think you may now find it's the other way around". Dad: "*expletive deleted* – I think you may well be right."
  I'd sailed 16 championships by then and countless Opens

- To a Royal Navy Captain, crewing for him with me: "Indeed the three most useless things to have on a sailing boat are 1) an umbrella stand, 2) a wheelbarrow, and 3) an Officer of Her Majesty's Navy".

- And one from his father (repeatedly) when, aged 11, I crewed for Dad. "I'll lend 'e me bicycle pump boy, then you might beat 'em."

Others
- You cannot win a race on the first beat, but you can lose it.

- In light airs, one side or the other will pay when a stronger breeze appears. Pick one and stick to the plan.

- It blows harder out of a blue sky.

- A spinnaker will always collapse when you take your eye off it.

- The sun will always be right behind the kite luff.

- You can often spot the line of tide on a channel by changes in water colour or texture.

- Sailing in bare feet is the route to a broken toe.

My RS200 crew
- One day when it was my turn at the front; "Why are you so crap?" A fair question perhaps, but not necessarily conducive to superior performance.

- On anther day "Can I helm?" followed by "So how do you gybe in big waves like these?" followed by "No, you helm" after we fell in.

A note about Paul Elvstrøm – why do I refer to him as the greatest dinghy sailor when our own Ben Ainslie is virtually untouchable? Well how about this: Paul won four consecutive Olympic Gold medals, in Fireflies in 1948 and in the Finn after its introduction in 1952. He sailed in eight Olympics, opting to be only a reserve in 1964, sailing thereafter in Star (finishing fourth), Soling and Tornado (twice). He missed bronze in the Tornado by only one point in 1984, aged 56, and competed again aged 60.

He also won 15 world championships in an unsurpassed eight classes: Finn (three), Star (three) 505 (two) where he helmed from the trapeze, Soling (two), Quarter Tonner (two), Snipe, FD and 5.5 metre (all one each). Then there were eight European, five Scandinavian and six Danish titles although he never sailed the Danish Finn Nationals because he would have won too easily.

He devised the ratchet block, the now universal self-bailer, weight jackets, buoyancy aids as we know them, flexible core-and-sheath ropes, radial-cut sails and non-skid soles for sailing footwear. He invented the hiking bench so he could train himself to hike harder than anyone else. For several years, his secret weapon was a 'kicking strap', which he fitted and removed while afloat before others finally cottoned on and it became ubiquitous. That is probably six, perhaps seven things you use every time you sail, all attributable to this one man.

All this at a time when sailing was strictly an amateur sport and there was still a need to earn a living by other means. Paul funded his racing career from his own house-building business.

He was also a key contributor to our rules, devising the two-length zone at marks and his rule books have helped thousands over generations. He was a key part of the debate that led to the introduction of the 49er at the Sydney Olympics.

A FEW HANDY TRICKS AND TIPS

HOW TO...

Call a layline: A good trick for a windward layline is to look over your aft-facing shoulder – if you can just see the mark in your peripheral vision, you are about there.

Tell if you will cross them: if more land or boats are becoming visible around the front of a converging boat, you are ahead – just make sure you are sufficiently ahead. Conversely, if more and more appears behind them, they are ahead of you. Keep checking though – a small windshift can make a big difference.

Tell if you are overlapped: it is hardly perfect, but there have been times when I have slid to the back of the boat and theatrically sighted along the line of the transom and given a nod or shake of the head. Remember the onus in the rules – if someone insists upon 'room', you are required to give it – then protest if you must.

Know where the start line is: The trick is transits. Some fixed start-lines are based on transits that you should be able to see. In this instance, check any inner or outer distance marks are on the line. If in front, sailing to them could put you over if the OOD is doing their job properly. If much more than a boat width behind the line, in theory they fail in their task and you could start beyond if you wanted. Remember that no one likes a smart Alec though. If there are no formal transits available, sail beyond the end(s), particularly the starboard end and try to find a transit yourself. Remember to adjust for the fact there may be several feet of boat in front of your viewing point.

Decide whether to duck or tack when on port tack: always an interesting one – like chess this can be taken to several levels. First question is, strategically and tactically speaking do you want to keep going or tack back? There needs to be a very good reason to let the traffic compromise your strategy. Second question is whether a duck will lose you a few inches or a couple of boat lengths? Third question: are you converging with an 'adult' who might let you cross if it means you do not tack and slow them down **or** someone inexperienced or small-minded who will insist on their 'rights' even if it hurts them? If you can virtually cross them, ask if you can keep going. But remember, if you are on port the onus is still on you to keep clear – they do not have to respond.

Next; if you decide to tack, make sure you do not get rolled or lose your freedom to tack in the future when you will want to. If they are on the layline, finding you are trapped and unable to make the mark yourself can be expensive. Better to be safe, further to the right in guaranteed clean air.

If it is all nip-and-tuck, perhaps approaching the finish, all other things being equal I would always choose to control the right because when you next converge you will have the benefit of being on starboard.

Tell if the kicker is too tight or too loose: A really good rule of thumb is to play the kicker until the last third of the top batten is parallel with the boom. You can then fine-tune so that the leech tell-tale at that batten is breaking around fifty per cent of the time.

Do bear in mind that sometimes, in some boats, this is an unobtainable ideal. In a Laser for example, the priority upwind is to pull the kicker/mainsheet tight enough in light airs to bend the mast and take up the luff-round cut into the sail. The tension required to achieve this will always hook the leech. That's why Laser sailors rarely have leech tell-tales. It would be too depressing.

Tell if your boat is absolutely upright: It will probably feel as if it is heeled to windward! If the rig is set up properly, the helm should feel neutral with no lee or weather helm. If in doubt, fit an inclinometer. After a while, you will find it has taught you what upright truly feels like – probably not what you believed before.

Make your sails last: Never leave them up and flapping when not sailing. Sails are made of fibres running at right angles to each other, with a layer of filler (Dacron/Nylon) or film applied (Mylar) to fill the gaps. Flapping shakes out the filler or damages the film. So keep jibs rolled around themselves until the last minute. Drop mainsails or, in boats like Lasers, keep the mast down or roll the boat on its side until you need it.

When your supplier has a sale on (winter is a good time), invest in a new sail and keep it for best. After a while, you should have a really good one (for the club Open or big club races) a decent one for club races and a clapped-out one for practice or 'blowing-dogs-off-chains' windy days.

Keep your spinnaker like new: Never leave spinnakers up flapping to dry. Lay them over the boat or wait until they can hang in the garage. If it is blowing old boots and you are likely to use it as a fishing net at some point, use an old one.

When the sail starts to lose that slippery 'new' feeling, apply a nono-technology finish like Holmenkol Seal'n'Glide. Not cheap, but far cheaper than a new sail.

Improve your boat handling: Identify the aspect that needs work most (tacks, gybes, hoists, mark roundings, whatever).

Go out on a nice gentle force-2 day, with no time pressure.

Divide the manoeuvre into discrete component steps. Going as slowly as you can, work through each step, aiming for consistency and a smooth flow between movements. As an example, this might even mean drawing an outline around the ideal place(s) to put your feet with a Magic Marker and aiming for those marks. If something is not flowing, examine a different method until you are happy. In tacks and gybes, movements should be mirror images. If the move is not correct for your weaker hand, it won't be right for your stronger one either.

Now you have the process broken down into repeatable steps, you can gradually speed up to normal pace, then step up to stronger breezes where the emphasis may change but the fundamentals will likely be the same.

It can help to vocalise each step too, whether single-handed or working with a crew. Something like "and-wait-two-three" before you cross in a roll-tack for example.

Having someone knowledgeable to watch or even film you from a coach boat will also be seriously helpful. If you are on safety-boat duty yourself, follow (without slowing them up!) a hotshot and observe closely what they do. Then let the muscle memory imitate them á la the Inner Game.

Prevent the boat creeping forward so much whilst trying to hold station on the start line: Let the kicker right off. Even with the mainsheet slack, a tight leech will hold air and power in the sail. Fully battened mainsails have a similar effect that you cannot really switch off - so you may need to modify your start line tactics.

Avoid three catastrophic boat speed killers:

1. Check slot gaskets regularly – fix them as soon as they look dodgy.

2. Broken rubber tiller universal joints – never store them bent over. Check regularly. It is really hard to sit out without an extension.

3. Weed - keep checking those foils. Tune in for vibrations felt through the tiller extension. Glance at the board on every roll tack.

See into the future:

- Read the weather forecast – preferably **not** from the Met Office. Try windfinder.com or xcweather.co.uk

- Look up and think about the clouds.

- Read the tide tables. Look at a tidal atlas.

- Use history – keep a logbook – it could make you look like a magician.

Learn the lessons of the past: I mention above keeping a logbook. You do not have to be as comprehensive as Dr Stuart Walker, but if someone pulled a trick on you, or vice versa, note it down. When we sailed the RS200, we had a special Facebook identity only the two of us could access that we used as a logbook and to discuss things. It worked well although if you are a computer nerd, a Cloud-based database would be better. Just remember to go back and read it now and then or most of that knowledge will be wasted.

Part 7
Final Thoughts

No, I don't want you to draw any conclusion. I want you to listen to what I just said
Joe Morgan

THE ONE UNWINNABLE BATTLE

Most club-sailors have a common enemy who is destined to win every single time. No, not the taxman, but ageing. I repeatedly tell my kids that age is an attitude, and to a large extent it is. Just as well too, given the age profile of club sailors in this country. Without the baby-boomer demographic I suspect the numbers taking part in our sport would be decimated. A generation or three ago, most would have retired from sport in their forties: not us, thankfully.

So age is an attitude – and that attitude is to go down fighting, on our own terms, to stay in the game for as long as we can; with a little homework, which I have done for you, we can know roughly what shots are going to get thrown at us.

The bad news is that from our mid-30s, and particularly from our 50s, heart walls thicken, reducing blood flow and similar effects happen to lung capacity. Muscle mass also tends to decline. So aerobic capacity and strength are reduced. Pertinently for sailors, our sense of balance declines too, which explains a few things for me. We also tend to put on weight up to about the age of 60, then start to lose it again. Injury recovery times extend, including the self-inflicted injury of that extra glass in the pub.

Although inevitable, these are not absolute. A sedentary overweight smoker of 32 can be less capable than someone in their late 50s who is neither of those things. My research into the research suggests that being active and making an effort to be aerobically fit can stave off these effects. Going dinghy sailing in itself helps and could make us live longer. How's that for an excuse to go sailing?

It is not all bad news. Research into ageing in the work place also identifies that as we get older we:

- Work harder and more effectively (substitute the word 'play' for 'work')
- Think before acting
- Have better interpersonal skills (good for crew relations)
- Have better motivation
- Have more experience and knowledge.

I would add patience and tolerance to that list and we can use both to our advantage, as we get longer in the tooth.

One of the great things about sailing is that it is not just about fitness, strength and a specific technique in the way that swimming or rowing are. We do not have to do lots of boring physical training to be a club-sailor. Keeping active obviously helps but is not a prerequisite.

Nevertheless, there are some things we should think about that most of us do not. Firstly, hiking technique; a key cause of sailing injuries is poor hiking posture, resulting in damage to knees and backs in particular. If you suffer from pain in either after sailing please try to establish the root cause. An adjustment in the way you hike, a change in toe-strap length or position or even a change in boat may be wise. Alternatively, try Pilates to build up your core-strength.

Secondly, warm up and do some stretching before each race. I have neglected to do this for virtually all of my sailing life. As a result I possibly have the world's tightest hamstrings and calf muscles, having spent so much time putting them under tension. Do not do that or if you already have, book a session with a physio to knead out the knots in your muscles and give you some exercises to work on. The good thing about stretching exercises is that you can do them virtually anytime and should not feel like you need a shower and change of clothes afterwards.

Thirdly, think about the story of the hare and the tortoise. Use your energy wisely, making sure you have enough in reserve to go all-out at key pinch points around the race-track such as starts and mark roundings.

If you are lucky enough to still be young, do not be complacent please! Time flies, so look after yourself and you will be more competitive for longer. That may not matter to you now but it will all too soon.

THE FUTURE

Four gold, one silver and one bronze medal at Beijing (from 11 classes), three-times leading the Olympic medals table – sailing in the UK is surely in rude health?

Well, yes and no. While it is great to see team GBR do so fantastically well at the games and elsewhere, shouldn't success lead towards sailing as a sport flourishing at club level? Shouldn't we be seeing people of all ages flocking to get involved in this, the ultimate participative sport?

I don't know about you, but I do not see this happening. Attendances at championships, opens and club races are not what they used to be when I was young(er) although part of that arises from the dilutive effect of having lots of new classes. Many clubs have substantial generation gaps, with strong youth sailing, the post-war baby-boomers now in their 40s, 50s and above, but a real paucity in the middle.

The real concern here is that a majority of our youth sailors are being lost to the sport and do not appear to come back. This should concern us all greatly. If we cannot fix it, sailing clubs are going to inexorably decline and die, leaving just a small clique. This would be a disaster, but the writing is there on the wall if we only look.

I understand all the arguments about competition for time and attention, schools discouraging the competitive spirit so everyone has to be 'a winner', the emphasis on 'elf-n-safety' and the rest. But I do not think they are the nub of the issue.

I contend that the driver of our Olympic success is also a key factor of decline in grass-roots club sailing and a major cause of our missing generations. Much of that Olympic success derives from the zone squad system. Clearly, such hot-housing creates champions, but what about the other 99.99%? Does going into a pressurised, school-like atmosphere engender a love of sailing as a pastime for life? Or does that approach virtually guarantee that sailing is dropped just as algebra might be after that final Maths exam?

Don't get me wrong, I love team GBR winning medals. But there is an adage I use in business that says 'what gets measured, gets done', with a vital collorary that 'what does not get measured does not get done'. Is the focus on medals (measured) distracting attention from grass roots sailing (less measured, if at all).

If so, that would be a great shame and a huge missed opportunity. Sailing is a sport that can be enjoyed by all. Race at whatever level you like, cruise, potter, in yacht or dinghy, on puddles, big lakes or the sea, regardless of gender, size or anything else, and all through your life, from cradle to grave.

So what is the remedy? I believe it starts at club, grass-roots level. We should be straight with our kids about the options and not try to live vicariously through them. If they do take a pop at the ultimate prize, we should work **harder** at managing their exit when the time comes (as it surely will for all but a tiny minority) than we do chauffeuring them around the circuit. We should be teaching them to evaluate whether more input-effort is translating to more fun and satisfaction for them. We should show them that here are lots of classes that are more friendly, more fun to sail than the Olympic boat-hierarchy, more affordable, more sociable. Classes where the racing is just as tight and probably far more enjoyable than the five-ring circus. Witness the phenomenon that is the RS200 class.

As clubs, we also need to be more welcoming to newcomers of all ages and skill levels. Why, in this day and age of competition for leisure time, do we believe we can justify charging a *joining* fee, when local gyms and social clubs offer free membership trials and other inducements? Then we expect newbies to acquire a boat (how do they choose wisely?) and some sailing kit. Instead, clubs should be establishing lease-fleets. Our teaching establishment need to come up with a qualification that truly demonstrates the holder is capable of taking out a lease-boat and not getting themselves, others or the boat into harm or danger. I am not convinced the current badges deliver this. Then we should recognise that being able to sail does not mean competitive in club-racing. There is an intimidating learning curve still to climb, but how many clubs have race-coaches and run start-racing courses?

Within our clubs, we need to break the age-divide; the old sea-dogs need to embrace any youngsters or newcomers into the fold and certainly not resent what they consider as intrusion into their on-going weekly rivalry with old Bill, against whom they have been slogging around those same cans for 30 years. In return hopefully the younger generation will see that we have picked up a valuable trick or two along the way.

We know ours is the ultimate sport, so should we accept that only a tiny minority of the population sails? Or should we be finding ways to get more involved? At the outset I suggested that a sign of madness was repeating a course of action but expecting a different outcome. In settling for this status quo, perhaps we are all mad after all.

GLOSSARY

Buddy	A more experienced sailor to provide friendship, support, guidance and advice
ISAF	International Sailing Federation, the governing body for the sport of sailing. The letter A is an anachronism. It would be ISF but there were lots of organisations called ISF already when it transmogrified from the IYRU (International Yacht Racing Union) in 1996
Kite	Spinnaker, whether symmetrical or an asymmetric
Lay-line	Imaginary line at which it is possible to make the next mark without needing to tack (or gybe) again
Left shift	A windshift where the wind blows more from the left, gauged from the direction the boat is heading
NLP	Neuro-Linguistic Programming
OCS	On Course Side. Over the line at the start or during when a one-minute rule is in force
Pinch-point	A pivotal moment where an inch or two gained or lost now (say to gain an overlap) could translate to many boat lengths in a couple of minutes time
Right shift	A windshift where the wind blows more from the right, gauged from the direction the boat is heading
Rhumb line	Shortest line connecting two marks of the course
RRS	Racing Rules of Sailing
RYA	Royal Yachting Association, sailing's UK governing body
Soak	Sailing as deep as you can on off-wind leg
TLC	What every boat deserves – Tender Loving Care
VMG	Velocity Made Good. Progress towards the next mark

APPENDIX 1
RACE LOGBOOK

Venue		Date	
		Start time	
Course		Race type	
Wind direction		Race category	
Wind strength			
Sea state		Boat sailed	
		Sails used	
Tide state		Crew	
HW/LW time			
		No. of starters	
Noteworthy competitors		Final position	

Lessons learned	

Maintenance issues	

Other comments	

APPENDIX 2
FINAL SUMMARY

1. Build some new, improved habits.

2. Prioritise and adapt.

3. Do not mix 'jobs for body' and 'jobs for brain'.

4. Join in at the start. This means still being in the front rank 30 seconds **after** the start. So find a clear lane, preferably with freedom to tack.

5. Keep your head out of the boat. Be aware of what is happening across the course. In the process, make you own good fortune.

6. Keep doing the right thing, going the right way, relentlessly. Stay positive, always.

7. Keep going until the finish line is crossed - be relentless. Do not choke.

8. Inject intensity bursts at pinch points such as starts, mark roundings and the finish line. Hike like crazy when it matters most.

9. Keep the boat moving – be where the breeze is.

10. Get the five essentials right, every second.

   - Sail trim
   - Course sailed
   - Balance. Keep the boat flat flat flat.
   - Centreboard
   - Trim, fore and aft

Apply these ten rules, every time you sail and surely improved results will follow.

FURTHER INFORMATION

Club Sailor: back to front available:

In paperpack form

As an Ebook

For Kindle Readers

For news and details see **www.clubsailor.co.uk**

Feedback and enquiries welcome to clive@eplett.co.uk

Also visit **clubsailor.co.uk** for

Clive's boat bimbles

Tips on sailing at Frensham Pond or in Lasers

The Vocabulary of Wind

Published by levium books

Lightning Source UK Ltd.
Milton Keynes UK
UKOW020039220212

187720UK00001B/4/P